AFGHAN HINDUS AND SIKHS

HISTORY OF A *THOUSAND* YEARS

INDERJEET SINGH

Readomania

Readomania
An imprint of Kurious Kind Media Private Limited
readomania.com
contact@readomania.com | Facebook: @iamreadomania |
X: @iamreadomania | Instagram: @iamreadomania

Reprinted in 2025
First Published in 2019 by Readomania

Edited by Indrani Ganguly

ISBN: 978-93-858543-8-5

Typeset in Palatino Linotype by Shine Graphics
Printed in Delhi

Cover sketch of the Gurdwara Sahib made from a photograph by Pritpal Singh.

Readomania

India has traditionally been the land of storytellers and a lot of us have an inherent skill of creating good plots, good stories and good narrations. With a little encouragement and support, many more authors will be widely read and attain a place in the sun. This is the essence of *Readomania*—an initiative that nurtures emerging stars of the literary world.

It would not be an exaggeration to say that *Readomania* is the talent hunt in fiction. It goes a step beyond by not just identifying the talent but also nurturing it and showcasing it to the world. In the process, we have created a powerhouse of content.

Readomania has four principal interest areas—traditional print publishing, online library of short stories and poetry, literary events and products.

The print publishing works towards delivering good quality content to the readers. We publish good authors in meaningful anthologies, novels and works of narrative non-fiction. Our books stand out for their perspectives, the plots, the language and most importantly their ability to enrich lives.

Take a break, read something nice, write something beautiful. Read our books or visit us at www.readomania.com and enjoy a whole new world of literature.

Dedicated to the resilience of the
Afghan Sikhs and Hindus.

Cities with Afghan Hindus and Sikhs

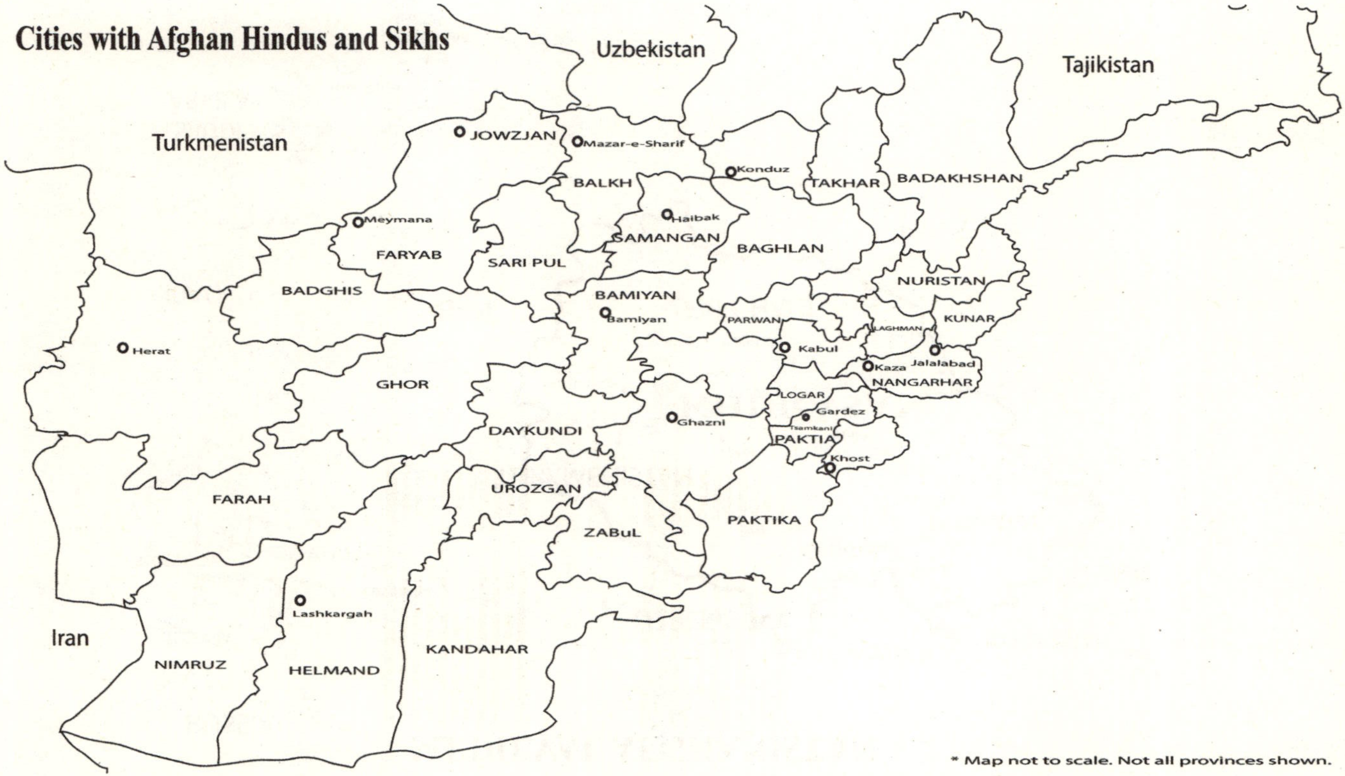

* Map not to scale. Not all provinces shown.

MEDIEVAL AFGHANISTAN

CONTENTS

Foreword

During my childhood, my father Sardar Teja Singh Khurana Ji used to tell me that we were Afghani Sikhs and have been living in this country for many generations. When I enrolled in the government school, the Muslim students questioned me, 'What are you, Hindi (Hindustani) Sikhs doing in our country? Why don't you go back to your own country?'

This gave birth to a number of intriguing questions in my mind. Who are we? Are we ethnic Afghani? What is our background? And, if we are refugees from India, why did our elders decide to settle in an Islamic country to lead a very challenging life?

In my youth, in addition to my academic education, I tried to find answers to these questions by speaking to elderly Sikhs in Afghanistan. In the midst of many agreements and disagreements, I was able to procure a lot of information about the history of my great nation, Afghanistan. During this period I had the good fortune of meeting the notable historian and writer, Sadhu Singh Saathi Ji and with him, I had the opportunity to contribute to his work, *Itihas Khalsa Diwan Afghanistan* which revolutionised the study of Afghan Sikhs and also inspired many others to study about them.

Later, Sardar Khajinder Singh Khurana Ji wrote *Kabul de Sangat te Afghanistan da Sankhep Ithas*. A little later, I in collaboration with Bhai Jodh Singh Maskeen Ji took up the task to write the modern history of *Khalsa Diwan Afghanistan* but due to various reasons, this work could not be published.

In 2012, when *Khalsa Diwan Afghanistan* was registered as a charity in the UK, I had the privilege to be one of the founding members along with Saathi Ji. After the formation of the charity, I requested Saathi Ji that we should document the history of prominent Sikhs living in different provinces of Afghanistan, their culture and customs, along with the history of the Gurdwaras in those provinces. However, Saathi Ji was at that time working on a book based on the *Dasam Granth* to clear the misconceptions facing the Panth. He assured me that we would begin the project proposed by me in 2014. But this was not to be. Saathi Ji was taken ill soon after, and joined the eternal light on 15th August 2015.

Subsequently, I thought that with Dr Raghbir Singh Bir of Afghan Medical Association of America, I will be able to write something meaningful but when I met him I realised that he too, was unwell and recovering from an illness which dashed my hopes.

In 2015, I met Sardar Harbans Singh Bewas Ji again; we had been introduced back in 2002 for the first time. I asked him if he was still writing and whether he would like to help me in the future. Bewas Ji replied that as long as he lives, he is dedicated to writing for the community and that his zeal to write will never diminish. This encouraging reply from an octogenarian rekindled my hope to finally produce a document about Afghan Sikhs. We got together and in 2017 started working on a book titled *Afghanistan de Sarzameen te Chooldey Nishaan aate Sikhi da Parvesh*. In addition to it, we have produced small booklets like *Saachi Succhi Kamaiye, The Report of Second Conference of Charity Khalsa Diwan Afghanistan, Sanjah Paigham, Dharam aate Bandagi* and *Das Dahake de Sewadar*.

It was during this period that I received a call from Inderjeet Singh. After saying his Gurfateh the caller introduced himself and said that he has written a number of articles on Punjab and Sikh history on Sikhnet.com, and is currently writing a book on the history of Afghan Sikhs and Hindus. He further said that he would like to meet me regarding this venture. We decided to meet on 7th April 2018 as he lived in Nottingham, about 130 miles north of London. I was very excited about the meeting but unfortunately, my younger sister passed away in the interim and we had to cancel our meeting.

However, Inderjeet continued with his work and contacted me again in August and we arranged to meet on Sunday, 26th August 2018 with Sardar Harbans Singh Bewas Ji as well. The meeting lasted for two whole hours and we exchanged many interesting thoughts. Inderjeet informed us that his book traces the history of Afghan Hindus and Sikhs from 10th century CE onwards. I was very pleased that someone was writing about us in the English language, for the very first time. I volunteered to write a foreword for the book which was readily and gratefully accepted by him.

We all know that our Shabad Guru is *Siri Guru Granth Sahib Ji* which guides us to lead a truthful life but sadly every scholar of our Granth has expressed their deep disappointment that Sikhs have not shared the enlightenment of our great Granth with the rest of the world. We are spending millions of rupees on gold plating the domes of the Gurdwara Sahibs but have been poor in spreading the message of *Siri Guru Granth Sahib Ji*.

In the same way, the Afghan Sikhs have a beautiful history and are ardent followers of the Sikh religion but have been unable to share and spread the information regarding their background in Afghanistan. Due to this negligence, the Afghan Muslims consider Afghan Sikhs as Indians and the Indians consider us as Afghans. In the post-1992 era we became refugees and faced huge difficulties in explaining our separate identity to the world. When Afghan

Sikhs applied for refugee status in the UK and the rest of Europe as our lives were in danger in Afghanistan, the officials told us that they had never heard of Sikhs from Afghanistan. Sadly, we got so involved in our businesses and modern lifestyle that we forgot to explain our separate identity to the rest of the world.

I had thought that after writing the complete history of Afghan Sikhs in Punjabi, I would translate it in English for readers in the UK, Europe and America so that they became more aware of the Afghan Sikhs. But this is not an easy task as a refugee, like the rest of my community, I too faced a number of issues and problems.

It is said that God does not go everywhere but sends his Saints instead, and I could see that my very old wish was being fulfilled by one such, Inderjeet Singh. He has painfully collected contemporary material on Afghan Hindus and Sikhs starting from 10th century CE and divided different centuries into separate chapters and brought little-known facts and facets of the life of Hindus and Sikhs in Afghanistan.

Inderjeet is an Amritdhari Sikh, a researcher who writes using contemporary sources and puts forward his diverse viewpoint in a way which does not offend anyone. He avoids controversies and creates a rapport with others very quickly. He gave me a summary of the chapters in his book which generated a lot of interest within me. I am eagerly waiting for his book to get published.

After going through the synopsis of each chapter, I believe that this is a unique work which could be used as a historical reference book on Afghan Hindus and Sikhs. In addition, this will be the first work on the history of Afghan Hindus and Sikhs in English and would be able to explore the separate identity and background of my people. I am sure readers in the UK, Europe, India, America, Canada and Afghanistan will find it equally interesting. I hope this book will be helpful for future works on Afghan Sikhs and Hindus.

I, Joginder Singh Khurana, Bewas Ji, our charity *Khalsa Diwan Afghanistan UK* and the Afghan Sikh community appreciate the hard work undertaken by Inderjeet Singh and wish him *Chardi Kala,* good health and a *Gursikhi* life so that he continues to share his research on Sikhs with the rest of the world.

I have full faith that this book will be a huge success and a milestone among Afghan Sikhs and Hindus just like the TV documentaries on our community produced by Bobby Singh Bansal and Pritpal Singh. I hope this work will inspire others to read and research on Afghan Sikhs and Hindus and make the rest of the world wiser about our separate identity.

As a former member of the Afghan Grand Assembly, I wish Inderjeet Singh all the best for the success of this book and sincerely hope that readers will like this unique work.

DR JOGINDER SINGH TEJ KHURANA
Former Member of Afghan Grand Assembly
London
April 2019

Preface

North Indian history as a subject always had an affinity with me during school days but after schooling, like most students in the sub-continent, I took the subjects which gave me better career prospects and unfortunately, history did not fit the bill.

In the next twenty years, I read a few books pertaining to history but never made any great effort beyond scratching the surface. In 2015, however, I discovered a Pakistani guy uploading his short videos and photographs about the little known Sikh heritage in West Punjab. This rekindled my interest in history and I joined *Facebook* to get in touch with him and his work. Shahid Shabbir, founder of the Pakistan Heritage Club and a celebrity due to his pioneer work, is the reason I rediscovered history. Soon, I started writing short articles for the *Sikhnet* website and within three years I had written over thirty articles. One of the articles on Zorawar Singh's campaign in Tibet in 1841 was enlarged and later published in *The Tibet Journal*. During this journey, our mutual friend Mirza Baig was also with us.

The next logical progression was to write a book. Like most of my articles, I am rather excited about working on a topic which has not been researched before or presents large gaps in our knowledge about it. The history of Afghan Sikhs and Hindus was one such topic. As a Sikh, I was worried that like the historical Gurdwaras left behind in Pakistan, the ones in Afghanistan may soon be abandoned.

Pritpal Singh made a huge name by producing, directing and anchoring the famous documentary, *Mission Afghanistan* and also televised programmes on the history of Afghan Sikhs in 2012. In February 2018, I approached Pritpal to ask him about his intentions on writing the history of Afghanistan considering his wide knowledge on the subject. Pritpal clarified that he was not interested in writing books though he had made another documentary on the Afghan Sikh and Hindu community. I then expressed my desire to write a journal or possibly a book on them and asked for his help and references.

Taking clues from Pritpal and his productions on the history of Afghan Sikhs, I managed to contact Khajinder Singh Khurana in New Delhi who had written a book on Afghan Sikhs in Punjabi in 2001. He was kind enough to send his book to me. Many months later, Harbans Singh Bewas Ji very kindly loaned his copy of the book written by the late Sadhu Singh Saathi to me.

I decided to write about the history of Afghan Hindus and Sikhs starting from the Hindu Shahi rulers who ruled Eastern Afghanistan until the end of the 10th century. The person who helped me make a start was Jahandad Khan. He is the scion of the Tanoli rulers of Hazara and a bright young man with a good sense of history. He provided me with references for the Ghazanavi and later periods. This assisted me immensely and I managed to find a number of contemporary sources.

During the course of the next six months, I studied and read a number of contemporary books which mentioned non-Muslims in Afghanistan from the 11th to the 20th centuries. I spoke to numerous Afghan Sikhs and Hindus across the globe. I am very grateful to Manmohan Singh (UK), Ram Saran Bhasin (Kabul) and Shamsher Singh (New Delhi) who provided details about the recent events in Afghanistan relating to Afghan Sikhs and Hindus.

I appreciate the support given by Ramnath Talwar (Belgium), Dr Chitra Akkor (USA), Dr Dalvir Pannu

(USA) and Gurpreet Singh Anand (India). I am grateful and feel honoured that Dr Joginder Singh Tej Khurana, former Member of the Afghan Grand Assembly, Afghanistan has written the foreword for this book. All people who have contributed towards this book have been duly acknowledged and mentioned in footnotes and references.

My special thanks to Vikramjeet Singh Roopai who shared his experiences about publishing and referred my name to the publishers. Indrani Ganguly, Dipankar Mukherjee and Rima Kar Ghosh from Readomania Publishing who have done a commendable job in producing this work.

I am thankful to all my family members who encouraged me especially Sardar Gurbux Singh who almost pestered me to write this book. Lastly, I express my gratitude to the academics, Dr Harbhajan Singh Soch, Former Vice Chancellor, Guru Nanak Dev University, Amritsar, Professor (retired) Himadri Bannerjee, Emeritus Professor Harbans Lal and Professor Akhtar H. Sandhu who encouraged me to keep on writing. Their words gave me confidence and the motivation to write.

This book is written in a semi-academic style using contemporary sources. I have resisted from providing any analysis and offering new theories as I want readers to form their own interpretations. This work can be used as a reference book and I hope this will prompt others to conduct further research on this little-known subject.

INDERJEET SINGH
Nottingham (UK)
April 2019

1

Introduction

The landlocked country of Afghanistan in south-central Asia was branded in India by the famous movie *Kabuliwala*. The image of a tall and handsome Punjabi, Balraj Sahni playing the role of a Pathan to perfection, and the haunting melody of Manna Dey's *Ay Mere Pyare Wataan Tuj Pe Dil Kurbaan* is etched on our minds. The movie was released in 1961, based on Rabindranath Tagore's short play by the same name. This represented Afghanistan to most Indians until the early 1970s.

However, ever since the late 1970s, Afghanistan has been in the news for all the wrong reasons. A relatively stable and peaceful monarchy was toppled by the cousin of the ruler in 1973 who was in turn, murdered in 1978. This was followed by the Soviet invasion in 1979 and to counter them came the Mujahideen (literally, freedom fighters) who were supported by the USA, Pakistan and their allies. The proxy war continued for ten years and by the time the Soviet left in 1989 after failing to crush the Mujahideen, the country was in shambles.

In 1992, just before the Mujahideen captured the capital, Kabul, the majority of the Afghan Hindus and

Sikhs had left the country. Four years later, the Taliban, a new version of the Mujahideen captured most of the country. Their rigid and fundamentalist interpretation of Islam meant that Hindus and Sikhs of Afghanistan had to wear a yellow batch to identify themselves. Although the Taliban has been replaced by a democratic government, the exodus has not stopped.

The Hindus and Sikhs of Afghanistan, who had been living in the country since time immemorial, left the land of their forefathers. While they numbered well over 60,000 in the early 1990s, only a thousand Sikhs and Hindus remain in the country presently and are limited mainly to the three cities of Kabul, Jalalabad and Ghazni. Outside these cities, their Gurdwaras and Mandirs are now illegally occupied by locals of the majority community. Even within these cities their houses were forcefully occupied during the turmoil of civil war and most of them live in Gurdwaras and Mandirs. They cannot even cremate their dead in Kabul and other provinces without the assistance of the police. Their children are bullied in schools, called *kafirs* and Sikh boys are mocked as *khachalu* (potato)[1]. This happens in front of the teachers and they don't do anything to discourage this behaviour. The worst and most hurtful is that they are continuously asked when they are going back to India. No one believes them when they say that they have always lived in Afghanistan. There has been a steep decline in the fortunes of this once rich and prosperous Afghan Hindu and Sikh community.

We have much in common with Afghanistan than we realise. The humble fruit, plum is known as *Aaloo*

Bukhara (literally, the potato from Bukhara). The city of Bukhara was a part of greater Afghanistan which was known as Khurasan. The Punjabi idiom, *Jo Sukh Chajjuu de Chaubare, Na Balkh na Bukhare* means that there is no place like home. However, the literal meaning is, 'the peace and tranquillity I find in my home at Chajju's Inn (Lahore) cannot be found in the big prosperous cities of Balkh (Afghanistan) and Bukhara (now, Uzbekistan). Babur, the Mughal who invaded India, joined Kabul and much of Eastern Afghanistan with North India, then known as Hindustan in 1526. He also brought melons from Afghanistan to India. Sarod, the stringed musical instrument is considered to have Afghan origins[2]. People, especially traders regularly travelled between the provinces of these two countries in the past two thousand years and even settled there, then why are Hindus and Sikhs not treated as natives of Afghanistan?

The Afghan Hindu community has now established Asamai Mandirs in India, Germany, England and USA, named after the famous Mandir in Kabul. Similarly, Afghan Sikhs have erected Gurdwaras in India and across Europe. The Guru Nanak Darbar in London is one such Gurdwara established by the Afghan Sikhs. The congregation in this Gurdwara had distinct Afghan facial features, especially the kids. Some of them had light-coloured eyes and even blonde eyebrows and eyelashes, one of the distinct Afghan traits that is difficult to ignore. In Afghanistan, some local Muslims refer to the Hindus and Sikhs as *Lala* which means elder brother. However, a significant number also discriminate against them. As a minority community in Afghanistan, the Hindus and Sikhs are considered foreigners whereas they are the original natives of the country.

This book is an attempt to trace the lives of Hindus and Sikhs in Afghanistan in the past thousand years. It is an effort to apprise the current and hopefully future generations on Afghan Hindus and Sikhs and about the journey of their ancestors. This is extremely important as almost 99 percent of all Afghan Hindus and Sikhs have now left the country.

Almost all history records, even those held by the Afghan Hindus stop at the Hindu Shahi rulers of Kabul in the 10th century and start again from the 19th century when European travellers and agents mentioned Hindus and Sikhs in the country.

This book has used contemporary sources as far as possible. At some places, eminent historians who are considered an authority on the subject have been quoted. Contemporary Persian, English, Punjabi sources have been used to chalk out references to non-Muslim communities including Hindus and later Sikhs from the 11th century to the 21st century. The contribution of these small communities of Hindus and Sikhs to the Afghan society is brought to the readers.

A number of theories are prevalent in Afghanistan to assert that the Hindus and Sikhs are recent emigrants to the country. Some of them are as follows:

1) Mahmud Ghaznavi, the infamous Sultan who invaded India seventeen times over a span of twenty-five years in the early 11th century brought thousands of Hindu slaves from India.

2) Babur joined Kabulistan with North India which led to the migration of Hindus from India to Afghanistan.
3) Sikhs and Hindus came to Afghanistan when Ahmed Shah Durrani (1748–72) brought merchants from Shikarpur (Sindh) and Multan (West Punjab).
4) Sikhs and Hindus came to Afghanistan in 1838 when the British and Maharaja Ranjit Singh deposed Dost Mohammed Khan and installed Shah Shuja at the throne.

This book begins from the 10th century when Islam had become the dominant religion in the country and will make the readers contemplate the above theories. Mahmud Ghaznavi's father won Kabulistan and replaced the Hindu Shahi rulers. He also replaced them in Peshawar and brought the infidel Ghor province under Islamic rule. Mahmud and his descendants had a significant number of Hindus in their army and administration.

Babur in his memoirs states that Kabul is Hindustan's own market. Indian merchants were trading in Kabul and other parts of Afghanistan even before Babur captured Kabul. Prior to him, the infidel Mongols ruled Khurasan, the greater Afghanistan and Timur in the 14th century fought many battles with idol worshippers who kept on attacking his capital Samarkand, part of Khurasan.

There were Hindu and Sikh merchants from Shikarpur and Multan in 18th and 19th century Afghanistan but in addition to them, the British accounts refer to local Hindus (and Sikhs) with families who lived in the different parts of the towns compared to merchants who lived among themselves without families in caravanserais.

British accounts of 1783 and 1808 refer to Hindu traders and shopkeepers in Kabul. Also, the Afghan Hindus and Sikhs are almost all from the Khatri and Arora castes that are renowned for their business acumen. The Jats form the majority in rural East Punjab and would have formed the bulk of armed forces under Maharaja Ranjit Singh. However, there is a complete absence of Jats among Afghan Sikhs (and Hindus) and same is the case with Sikhs in the Khyber Pakhtunkhwa province in Pakistan which borders Afghanistan and shares socio-cultural and tribal ties with each other.

Medieval Afghanistan was known as Khurasan, this was a greater Afghanistan as it included parts of present-day Uzbekistan, Iran, Tajikistan and Turkmenistan among others. However, during a major period in the medieval age especially from 1220 to 1748, the country was ruled by non-Afghan dynasties and was part of great empires (Mongols, Timurids, Mughals and Safavid) whose capitals were based outside present Afghanistan. Hence in this work, in some chapters especially for the above period (1220–1748), references are made to other major cities which were part of Khurasan but now fall outside Afghanistan. The provinces of Pakistan, namely Baluchistan and Khyber Pakhtunkhwa which share the border with Afghanistan have substantial Pashtun/Pathan population and also share major social, cultural and tribal ties with each other. Interestingly, the Hindus and Sikhs in these provinces have a number of similarities with Afghan Sikhs and Hindus. A separate chapter elaborates on these Pathan Sikhs of Pakistan.

Geographic location and major cities

Afghanistan is a landlocked country located in south-central Asia. Historically, it lay within the major trade routes and had its fair share of invasions mainly from western and northern Asia. Afghanistan borders six different nations and shares the longest border with Pakistan, almost the entire eastern and southern part, which is known as Durand Line drawn by the British regime in India. Afghanistan rejected the Durand Line when Pakistan was created in 1947 as Pashtun tribes lived across both sides of the border. Professor Ganda Singh who visited Afghanistan in 1951 reported a vibrant support for Pashtunistan (Land of Pashtuns). This issue is no longer emotive on that level, but it never died out much to the chagrin of Pakistan which has hosted millions of Afghan refugees since the 1980s.

Towards the west, Afghanistan borders the Shia-majority country of Iran. The Iran-based dynasties ruled major parts of Afghanistan in the medieval times until 1748 when Ahmed Shah Durrani created modern Afghanistan. In an ultra-conservative Sunni country with an almost 99.99 percent Muslim population, the Hazaras who are Shia and have partial Mongolian features are at the bottom of the class hierarchy.

Turkmenistan, Uzbekistan and Tajikistan share their borders with the country in the north. The shortest border is with China in far north-east which is just 76 kilometres long. The following cities and towns have been mentioned frequently in the book:

Kabul is the capital and largest city located in the eastern part of the country. It was the capital of Hindu Shahi rulers before rulers of the Ghaznavi dynasty won it in the 10th century. It became the capital of the country during the reign of Timur Shah Durrani in 1776. The city hosts more than half of the 1,000 Afghan Sikhs and Hindus still in the country and has a number of old and historical Gurdwaras and Mandirs.

Jalalabad is the capital of Nangarhar province in eastern Afghanistan. It was a leading centre of trade activity and is less than 100 miles away from Peshawar (Pakistan). The province had an appreciable number of Hindus and Sikhs. There were more than fifteen Gurdwaras in the province before 1992. In addition to Kabul, Jalalabad still has some Afghan Sikh and Hindu population who continue to look after the historical Gurdwaras and old Mandirs.

Ghazni in central Afghanistan rose to prominence when Sabuktigin made it the capital of the Ghaznavid Empire in the 10th century. The city was destroyed by the Ghurid dynasty that replaced the Ghaznavis as the rulers but was later rebuilt. Some would say that it never really regained the same prominence. A handful of Afghan Sikhs and Hindus live in the city presently.

Kandahar located in the south of the country is the second largest city. It was ruled by an 'infidel' dynasty known by the name of Zunbils until the late ninth century when it was conquered by Yaqub, the ruler of Persia. The Kandahar-based Hotak dynasty replaced the Persian Safavids in 1709 and ruled Persia, Afghanistan and the surrounding areas until 1738 when Nadir Shah defeated them. Within a decade the city was the capital of Ahmed Shah Durrani. It has been a stronghold of the Taliban in recent times.

Herat located in the western part of the country is the third largest city. In the medieval times, it was an important city of Khurasan, the region encompassing Persia, Afghanistan and Central Asia. Another important city of Khurasan which is now in northern Afghanistan was **Balkh**, known as Bactria in ancient times. It was an important seat of the Greco-Bactrian kingdom. The largest city of Balkh province is Mazar-i-Sharif. Within this region, **Kunduz** is another city which has gained importance in modern times.

Other major cities of Khurasan were **Mashhad** and **Nishapur**, now in north-eastern Iran and **Bukhara** and **Samarkand**, now in Uzbekistan. These cities were centres of trade but were destroyed by the Mongols and later devastated by Timur. Compared to the regions in Khurasan which embraced Islam in the seventh century, the south and eastern parts of modern Afghanistan took to the Muslim faith only from 9–11th centuries.

The semi-academic style of presentation in this book allows readers to enjoy the plain and free-flowing language without compromising on the references. The friends, Afghan Sikhs and Hindus who have helped in this venture have been mentioned throughout the book.

The book is dedicated to the resilience of the Afghan Sikhs and Hindus who are still living in Afghanistan and looking after the historical shrines which commemorate the visit of Guru Nanak in the country. It is a humble effort to make them and everyone else aware of their rich history, and hopes that some fellow Afghan Muslims will not consider them as outsiders and treat them as natives of Afghanistan.

References

1. Sikh boys cover their heads and tie a *patka* which shows their *joora* (refers to a bun, or topknot, of hair wound around and secured at the top of the head). The *joora* is referred derogatorily as *khachalu* by Muslim boys which means potato in Afghan languages.
2. Kahn Singh Nabha. (1930). *Gur Shabad Ratn Mahan Kosh.* Patiala.

2

Afghan Hindus under Ghaznavi Rulers in 11th and 12th Centuries

Sabuktigin (ruled 977–97) conquered Kabul and neighbouring areas from Jayapal, the Hindu Shahi ruler in 986 and later his son Mahmud of Ghazni (ruled 998–1030) won Peshawar in 1001. In the 11th century, Afghanistan ushered in the rule of the Ghaznavi rulers and a sea change in the social and religious dynamics of the provinces.

Mahmud of Ghazni (971–1030) was an infamous iconoclast who destroyed temples and idols, but he also had political motives for doing so in addition to the religious reasons. The Hindu temples were full of gold and jewels; hence, there were economic reasons to invade India frequently. It is said that he forcibly converted a lot of Hindus but like most other Muslim rulers he also allowed Hindus to live within his empire as *Dhimmi* (protected people) with some restriction and obligatory payment of *Jizya* tax. In addition to being employed in administration, Hindus also served in Mahmud's army and he used them very cleverly against his opponents.

Jabir Raza[1] quotes a contemporary work *Siyasat Namah* which states that Mahmud had Turks, Hindus, Khurasanis, Arabs, Ghurids and Daylamities (people who lived in Daylam Mountains in North Persia). These groups had their own regiments.

A contemporary source *Hudud Al Alam* gives us an indication of the extent of Islam in Eastern Afghanistan at this stage. This anonymous geographical work which means 'Regions of the World' was compiled in 372 AH or 982-83 AD and dedicated to Amir Abul Marith Mohd Bin Ahmed, the local ruler of Guzganan which is now part of Northern Afghanistan. The Russian Orientalist, Vladimir Minorsky translated it in 1937. The author was in the middle of revising the book when he died in 1966 and it was completed by renowned historian C.E. Bosworth and the second edition was published in 1970[2].

The work refers to a number of cities of Afghanistan, some of which had a non-Muslim majority at the time of writing have been put under Hindustan. The work corresponds with the reign of Sabuktigin (977–97), the founder of the Ghaznavid dynasty.

Wakhan (Badakhshan province): Several towns of Wakhan are listed and 'the last place in the limits of Transoxiana'[3] was a large village by name of Samarqandaq (Little Samarkand) where Hindus, Tibetans, Wakhanians and Muslims lived.

Ninhar (modern Nangarhar province): The work states that the king of Ninhar 'makes show of Islam' and had over thirty wives that included Muslims, Afghans and Hindus. The people were idolaters and there were three large idols in Ninhar.

Kandahar: Kandahar is described as a large town with numerous idols of gold and silver where hermits and Brahmins resided. It is described as a pleasant town of a special province.

Gardez: Gardez is described as a frontier town between Ghazni and Hindustan which was situated on the summit of a mound. The town had a strong fortress with three walls. The people were Kharijite Muslims.

Laghman: It is a town situated on the middle course of the river. We are told that it was an 'Emporium of Hindustan' and residence for merchants. The town had idol temples.

Parwan: It is narrated as a pleasant town and as the 'Gate of Hindustan'. The town was a 'resort of merchants'.

Wahind (KPK province, Pakistan): It was the capital city of Jaypala, the Hindu Shahi ruler, and the town had few Muslims. Merchandise from Hindustan such as musk and other precious things regularly came to this country.

Kabul: The city had a solid fort which was known for its strength. The inhabitants were Muslims and Indians[4] and there were temples with idols in the city. We are told that the ruler of Kannauj (Uttar Pradesh, India) made a pilgrimage to the temples of Kabul. Unlike the above towns and cities which are listed under Hindustan, Kabul is listed under Khurasan.

According to one of the theories denying native origin to Afghan Sikhs and Hindus, it is said that Mahmud brought a lot of Hindu slaves from mainland India marking their first entry into the country. However, it is highly likely that some of the Hindus who served under his administration and army were the natives of Khurasan and Kabulistan as these places had a substantial number of Hindus. The *Tarikh-e-Sabuktgin* by Abul Fazl al Baihaki refers to Hindus working in responsible positions under the Ghaznavi rulers[5].

Baihaki writes that fifty days after the death of Sultan Mahmud, his son and successor Masud dispatched Sewand Rai, a Hindu chief with a large Hindu cavalry to pursue the nobles who were supporting his rebel brother for the throne of Ghazni. In the subsequent battle, Sewand Rai and the majority of his troops perished but managed to inflict heavy losses upon their opponents.

The book then mentions that five years later, Tilak, son of Jai Sen, was the commander of Hindu troops in the service of Sultan Masud. He was sent to chastise the rebel chief Ahmad Nialtigin. Tilak chased the rebels and managed to capture thousands of them. Ahmad was killed while he was trying to cross the river by Jats (Hindu) at the behest of Tilak. To quote another contemporary source, the book *Tabakát-i Akbari* refers to Tilak as Malik bin Jai Sen[6].

Baihaki mentions another Hindu general by the name of Biji Rai who served under Mahmud but later left for Kashmir due to political dissensions. During the reign of Masud's successor, Abu Ali, the *Kotwal* (similar to the police chief or magistrate) of Ghazni, later commanded an army and maintained conquests in Hindustan (the Ghaznavi Empire to the east extended approximately to present-day Pakistan) wrote to Biji Rai and invited him to return to Ghazni.

Baihaki further states that Sultan Masud was drinking wine in the royal garden when he ordered a dispatcher to be sent to Tilak and ask him to advance against the rebel Ahmad Nialtigin. We are told that Tilak arrived at Lahore and took 'several Muslim prisoners who were the friends of Ahmad'. The right hands of the prisoners were cut off at the orders of Tilak which terrified them, and they pleaded for mercy and deserted Ahmad. Tilak then pursued Ahmad with a large number of troops, the majority of whom were Hindus, defeated Ahmad in a number of skirmishes and one full-fledged battle but Ahmad was able to escape each time. Tilak then wrote a letter to the Hindu Jat leaders that whosoever brought back Ahmad or his head would receive a reward of 500,000 dirhams.

Baihaki writes that this strategy worked and a number of Jats started pursuing Ahmad and once the rebel leader was crossing the river, two to three thousand Jats fell upon him who had less than 200 horsemen with him. Ahmad was killed and several men, including the son of the rebel, were taken captive and huge wealth fell into the hand of the Jats. Tilak was made aware that the Jats had acquired immense money and property from Ahmad so he asked them to forgo the reward money. After some negotiations, Tilak paid 100,000 dirhams in lieu of the head of Ahmad, his son and other captives at Lahore.

The Sultan was very pleased and 'expressed his obligations to Tilak and the others and praised them for their conduct'. This increased the prestige and status of Tilak in the court of Ghazni.

Baihaki further gives us an account of the extraordinary rise of Tilak, son of a barber, who 'was handsome in face and appearance and had an eloquent tongue' and wrote very well in Hindvi (Indian language) and Persian. He had lived in Kashmir for a long period of time. He was employed (in Ghazni) by Kazi Shiraz Bul Hasan who was so impressed by him that he 'restrained him from going anywhere else' (for employment). However, Tilak through a stratagem managed to find work under Khwaja Ahmad Hasan who made him his secretary and translator (between Khwaja and the Hindus). Baihaki writes that he saw Tilak performing the duties of secretary, interpreter and 'managing difficult affairs'.

Later, Tilak was appointed as an interpreter by Sultan Mahmud. He was 'a clever speaker' and 'rendered valuable service to Sultan' by bringing 'all the Hindu Kators and many outsiders under his rule'. For this (diplomacy) Tilak obtained great honours from the ruler.

During the reign of Shah Masud, Tilak was promoted to manage the affairs of Balkh in place of another Hindu general known by the name of Sundar. Tilak was given a 'gold-embroidered robe, hung a jewelled necklace of gold around his neck, and placed an army under him'. Baihaki adds, 'a tent and an umbrella were also given to him. Kettle drums were beaten at his quarters, according to the custom of the Hindu chiefs, and banners with gilded tops were granted.'

Tilak sat among the nobles in the privy councils and was employed in important duties. Baihaki pays his tribute to him, 'nobody is born great—men become such.

But it is important that they should leave a good name behind. This Tilak soon became a man and had excellent qualities. All the time he lived he sustained no injury on account of being the son of a barber. But if with such a character, wisdom, and spirit, he had been of good extraction, he would have been better, for nobility and talents are both very agreeable. But nobility is good for nothing if learning, propriety and spirit are wanting.'

Hindus and battle at Kerman

Another recorded instance displaying the presence of Hindus in the army was the battle of Kerman. Ahmad Ali Noshtigin along with a section of Hindu troops was fighting rebels in Kerman (Iran) and the latter 'would not advance and turned their backs in flight'. This created panic among the rest of the army which forced Ahmad to retreat. The Hindu troops fled to Sistan (Iran) and then returned to Ghazni.

Baihaki was an eye-witness to the ordeal the Hindu officers underwent at the Sadhazara garden in Ghazni. The Sultan (Masud) ordered them to be kept in a large house which was used as a despatch office. The accountant brought 'several severence orders from the Sultan' and the last one was that they (Hindu officers) were dismissed. Immediately, six of the officers committed suicide with their own daggers and blood started to flow into the office. Baihaki and the accountant informed Masud about it, who remarked that they should have used the daggers at Kerman instead. Baihaki adds that Masud treated them severely but forgave them in the end.

Baihaki writes that on the night of 18th March 1039 CE, ten Turkoman horsemen came near the royal garden during the night, plundered and killed four Hindu foot soldiers. These looters retreated to the neighbourhood of Kunduz where elephants were stabled and drove the animals away. A boy (perhaps son of one of the elephant riders) was sleeping on the back of the elephant and he was woken when they passed beyond the city. The boy was threatened with death if he did not ride the elephant faster, to which the poor child agreed. By morning the Turkoman horsemen had covered a great distance. When this was reported to the Sultan he chastised some Hindu elephant riders for negligence and ordered the price of the animal to be recovered from them.

Hindu physicians

Jabir Raza quotes the great Alberuni who writes that Hindu physicians were employed by the Ghaznavi rulers. For instance, when the chief of Gardez (Paktia province) was suffering from chronic piles, their Muslim physician despite using several medicines was unable to cure but a Hindu physician was able to cure it using an Indian aconite (plant)[7].

Ghor province

Tarikh-i-Guzida written by Hamdullah Mustaufi mentions that the people of the province of Ghor were infidels and ruled by a pagan chief by the name of Suri. Sultan Mahmud (998–1030) invaded Ghor and in the subsequent battle Suri was killed and his son was taken a prisoner who 'killed himself by sucking poison which he had kept under the stone of his ring'. The region was annexed, and the population was converted to Islam. It is interesting to note that the latter day Ghurids replaced the Ghaznavids in 1173 and became the rulers of modern Afghanistan, Pakistan and North India[8].

The Ghurids had their share of battles with infidels. Habibi (1967) mentions the battle of Sultan Muizuddin Mohammed 'against the infidels of Khata and the people of Turkestan' in Andkhoy (Faryab province, northern Afghanistan). We are told that the battle was led by Hussain Kharmail, chief of Garziwan (Faryab province) from the Ghurid side but was unable to make any progress and Malik Osman Samarkandi from the Al Afrasiab family of Turkestan negotiated and established peace between the two adversaries.

Sultan Muizuddin Mohammed is popularly known as Mohammed Ghori, best remembered in India for his two battles with Prithviraj Chauhan. Habibi adds that the Sultan was killed 'by a devotee of the infidels in Dameek (Jhelum district, West Punjab) on 14th March 1206[9].

It is fascinating to note that even during the reign of Mahmud of Ghazni, a big enclave of pagans lived and ruled in the Ghor province while being surrounded by Islamic states. We are not told if these pagans were Hindus or Buddhists by the contemporary works but modern historians continue to speculate their ethnicity and background.

The Hindus were a part and parcel of the society in the Ghaznavid Empire. They were in the imperial army and administration. Baihaki makes reference to separate quarters of Hindus in the capital, Ghazni, where they were allowed their religious ceremonies. Raza quotes Al Maari's *Risalat ul Ghufran* which describes the scene of the ritual Sati performed by a Hindu woman in Ghazni. The Italian Archaeological Mission in Afghanistan discovered a statue of Brahma in the excavations of a palace at Ghazni that was built by Sultan Masud III (1112)[10]. Raza states that this discovery 'clearly supports the fact that Hindu forms of worship were respected'.

References

1. S. Jabir Raza. (2011). *Hindus under the Ghaznavids* in *Proceedings of the Indian History Congress,* 71st Session, Malda 2010–11. Kolkata: Indian History Congress.
2. Vladimir Minorsky. (1970). *Hudud Al Alam 'The Regions of the World' A Persian Geography,* 372 AH–982 AD. 2nd ed. London: Messrs Luzac & Co.
3. Transoxiana means beyond the Oxus River (Amu Darya) in Central Asia.
4. It means Hindus (could include Buddhists).
5. H.M. Elliot and John Dowson. (1869). *The History of India as Told by its Own Historians: The Muhammadan Period.* Vol 2. London.
6. H.M. Elliot and John Dowson. (1869). *The History of India as Told by its Own Historians: The Muhammadan Period.* Vol 5. London.
7. Hakim Mohammed Said (Ed.). (1973). *Al-Biruni's Book on Pharmacy and Materia Medica.* Karachi.
8. H.M. Elliot and John Dowson. (1871). *The History of India as Told by its Own Historians: The Muhammadan Period.* Vol 3. London. The Ghaznavi province of Lahore was captured in 1186.

9. Abdul Hai Habibi. (1967). *A Short History of Afghanistan.* Kabul: Historical Society of Afghanistan.

10. A. Bombaci. (1959). 'Summary Report on the Italian Archaeological Mission in Afghanistan I: Introduction to the Excavations at Ghazni'. *East and West.* N.S. 10/1–2, pp. 3–22.

Notes

Political Legacy: Pakistan has named their hypersonic surface-to-surface short-range ballistic missile as *Ghaznavi* and medium-range ballistic missile, *Ghauri.* Another short-range surface-to-surface ballistic missile, the *Haft-II Abdali* has been named after Ahmed Shah Abdali (1748–72) who is considered as the founder of modern Afghanistan.

In 2006, Afghanistan formally complained to Pakistan for naming its ballistic missiles and other weapons after historic Afghan heroes and asked them not to link Afghan rulers' names with 'tools of destruction and killing'. Pakistan declined to change the names and argued that the two countries shared a common history. (http://news.bbc.co.uk/1/hi/world/south_asia/4740570.stm accessed on 23rd August 2018).

Modern translators have found few mistakes in Elliot and Dowson's work especially around names, but this has little effect on the theme of the chapter. (Islamabad-based Jahandad Khan Tanoli brought these contemporary sources to the attention of the author.)

3

Infidel Mongols, Rulers of Khurasan in 13th Century and Ibn Batuta's Early 14th Century Account

Mongols

The Mongols under Genghis Khan formed one of the biggest Empires in medieval ages and by 1220 CE the infidel, Genghis Khan had captured most of Afghanistan. For the next seventy-five years, the Afghans were ruled by the infidel Mongols. It is important that we mention infidel before Mongols here as most people assume that he was a Muslim as his last name was Khan. In truth however, his faith and those of the Mongols had little in common with the Abrahamic religions.

Genghis or Chinggis Khan (d. 1227) belonged to a religion which we now term as Shamanism. It is a religion characterised by belief in an unseen world of gods, demons, and ancestral spirits responsive only to the shamans (their priests)[1].

Around 1259 the Mongol Empire became fragmented and the kingdom comprising most of present-day Afghanistan, Iran, and Azerbaijan to parts of Turkey came to be known as Ilkhanate. During this period, it is considered that the Ilkhanate rulers were Buddhists or were sympathetic to Buddhism. In 1295, the Mongol ruler Ghazan converted to Islam and came to be known as Mahmud Ghazan. The next ruler Oljeitu, brother of Ghazan, is said to have accepted Shia Islam in 1310. The last great ruler of the Ilkhanate was Abu Sa'id Bahadur Khan and in the 1330s the kingdom was ravaged by plague and famine. The Khan himself died due to plague in 1335.

Even after converting to Islam, Mongols continued to follow the traditional practices of their former belief and did not stop their hostility towards other Muslim states like Egypt. It took them a considerable number of decades before they fully adopted the Islamic practices.

Minhaj al-Siraj Juzjani, a contemporary Persian historian who wrote the *Tabakat-i Nasiri*[2] around 1260, provides details of the Muslim dynasties in Central Asia. Juzjani records the invasion and annexation of Khurasan (modern Afghanistan) by the infidel Mongol Empire headed by Genghis Khan. The devastation of Central Asian cities including those in modern Afghanistan is mentioned in some detail.

Peter Jackson, an authority on Muslim dynasties in Central Asia during the medieval ages has written a very comprehensive book on the Mongols using varied sources[3]. Jackson writes that in addition to the extensive destruction, the local Muslim population experienced the infidel Mongol rule as alien or oppressive in five aspects in particular:

1) the importation of unfamiliar religious traditions that could not be reconciled with the Islamic dispensation;

2) the imposition of taxation that had no sanction in the Sharia;
3) the prohibition, in certain cases, of canonical Islamic practice or the enforcement of the steppe customs that were contrary to it;
4) the appointment of non-Muslim personnel to higher administrative offices; and
5) the even-handed treatment of all faiths (effectively entailing, therefore, a demotion of Islam from the previous commanding position).

Jackson quotes that Mahmud Ghazan and Oljeitu referred to God as 'Tenggeri rather than Allah in their correspondence with the Christian West' (States). In 1303, contemporary sources state that Ghazan celebrated the Mongol New Year. Ghazan, however, destroyed pagodas and Zoroastrian fire temples and replaced them with mosques and colleges. Churches were destroyed and *Jizya* was imposed on Christians but the ruler took a U-turn and abandoned discrimination of the Christians when he needed the support of the European states against the Egyptians.

Jackson writes that the Buddhists migrated into Ilkhanate (region included Afghanistan) in considerable numbers from China, Tibet and Kashmir after the Mongol conquest. The infidel Mongol rulers placed great confidence in Buddhist monks and built several pagodas. The earliest one seems to be at Labnassagut close to Alatagah. The Mongol ruler Gaikhatu was brought up as a Buddhist and remained so throughout his life. The remains of rock-cut Buddhist temples found near Maragha and Qongqur Uleng (both in North Iran) were built in this era.

Many infidel members of Hulagu Khan's (1218–65) lineage married Muslim princesses contrary to the Sharia as marriage to an infidel is forbidden. Sometimes these marriages led to more breaches of Sharia as Mongols continued to practice their laws which also allowed marriage to a widowed stepmother.

Genghis Khan did not invade India and the country escaped the fury and destruction by the Mongols. Consequently, we do not have any direct reference to Hindus in the contemporary history. However, India was the frontier to the Mongol Empire as they ruled over Afghanistan. The oldest surviving literary work in the Mongolian language, *The Secret History of the Mongols* written by a Mongol royal just after the death of the great Khan makes a passing reference to Hindus[4].

Verse 261 states that the Khan sent the Mongol commander Dorbei Doqshin to attack the cities of Herat, Merv (Turkmenistan) and Alamut (Iran), 'all of which lay between the lands of Hindu people and the Baqtat (Baghdad, Iran) people'. Herat in Afghanistan is close to the Iranian border hence according to this manuscript beyond Herat (on eastern side of Afghanistan) was the land of the Hindu people. Buddhists, Muslims, Shamanists and Christians lived under the Mongol rule. Hindus could well have lived in both Mongol and non-Mongol ruled regions of Afghanistan.

The Mongols were replaced by Timur in Khurasan in 1335 that caused a lot of destruction and devastation of the Muslim cities in Central Asia. Although Timur professed to be a follower of Islam, this did not stop him from destroying his opponents even if they happened to follow his religion.

Ibn Batuta's accounts—1331–32

Ibn Batuta, one of the prolific travellers and writers of the medieval era passed through Khurasan while on his way to Hindustan. Although he does not write about Hindus in the country, he does mention ascetics called Haidaria. The description is very similar to a sect of Nath Yogis in India.

Batuta praises the sweetness of the melon from Khwarazm (delta of Amu Darya). The fruit could be cut in oblong pieces and dried like figs and was carried to India and China and 'occasionally used as a present to their kings'. It was not uncommon at that time for people from Central Asia to come to India and vice-versa.

Batuta mentions that Balkh, Kandahar and Merv were in ruins then along with parts of Kabul. Batuta also gives an explanation behind the name of the Hindu Kush Mountains[5]. Herat was the largest populated city in Khurasan followed by Nisabur (Nishapur). Batuta writes that people of Herat were 'religious, sincere, and chaste' and followed the Hanifa school of Islam.

Batuta then went to Sarakhas followed by Zava, the town of Sheikh Qutbuddin Haider. Here, he saw a sect of fakirs known as Haidari named after the Sheikh. The ascetic group placed iron rings on their hands, neck and 'more strangely, on their virilia, in order to prevent intercourse with women'.

Batuta refers to the Hindu Kush as 'high mountains covered with snow and exceedingly cold'. The people refer to them as Hindu Kush meaning 'Hindu Slayer' because the majority of slaves brought here from Hindustan died due to the intense cold conditions.

Batuta writes that Kandahar was once a big city but stood ruined then and Kabul was in a similar state as well. Batuta states that the city of Kabul is populated by people from Persia who are called 'Afghans'. The mountains in the region are difficult to access and have narrow passes. He adds that the Afghans were 'powerful and violent people' and that most of them were 'highway robbers'.

Batuta expressed relief and thanked God when on the way from Kabul to Kirmash they managed to escape from being robbed in a narrow pass between two mountains where robbers were shooting arrows from the heights of the mountain.

Batuta writes that they arrived at Shish Naghar which is 'situated at the extremity of the Turkish dominions'. From here they entered 'the great desert' and after fifteen days they reached Panj Ab (five waters) safely. He adds that this was the 'junction of five different rivers' and provided water for agriculture in the province. Batuta mentions that they comfortably got on to the river at the beginning of the month of Moharram, 734 AH (1332 AD).

Reference

1. *Merriam Webster Dictionary.*

2. Maj. H.G. Raverty (Trans.). (1881). Tabakat-i Nasiri: *A General History of the Muhammadan Dynasties of Asia including Hindustan from AH 194 (810 AD) to AH 658*

(1260 AD) and the Irruption of the Infidel Mughals into Islam by Maulana Minhajuddin Abu–Umar-I-Usman, London.

3. Peter Jackson. (2017). *The Mongols and the Islamic World from Conquest to Conversion,* London: Yale University Press.
4. Urgunge Onon. (2001). *The Secret History of the Mongols: The Life and Times of Chinggis Khan.* London: Routledge.

   Verse 264 states that Khan spent seven years among the Sarta'ul (Muslim) people. While Khan was there, Commander Bala Cherbi 'crossed the Shin River and pursued both Jalaldin-soltan (last ruler of the Khwarezmian dynasty) and Qan-Melik to the lands of the Hindus. Cherbi was unable to find them 'even though he searched right into the heart of the lands of the Hindus'.
5. Samuel Lee. (1829). *The Travels of Ibn Batuta,* London: J Murray.

Notes

Professor Charles Melville of the University of Cambridge in his lecture paper presented on 12th March 1997 at the University for the Indo-Mongolian Society of New York titled *The Impact of the Mongol invasions on Iran, Iraq and Central Asia: A Revaluation* quotes from a 14th century manuscript that during the third attack on Merv (now in Iran but was part of Khurasan) around 1222, the Mongols carried widespread torture for forty days and only 'a hundred souls survived this'. In the end, only ten or twelve Indians were left residing in the city. One may speculate they may have been traders or residents of the city but it is worth noting that there were Hindus living in Merv even in 1222.

4

Timur and Infidels in 14th–16th Century Accounts

Timur (1336–1405) was one of the greatest conquerors and founder of the Timurid Empire which included Afghanistan, Persia and Central Asia. His battles and campaigns against the idol worshippers and infidel Jats in Central Asia make it imperative to discuss him in some detail. He also invaded Hindustan in 1398 and sacked Delhi which was then under a weak Tughluq ruler who fled away. The Hindu and Muslim chiefs tried to defend the city but were no match to one of the most powerful armies at the time. Timur's rule (1370–1405) and campaigns caused many deaths and most of his victims were fellow Muslims. Mohammad Habib and K.A. Nizami[1] refer to him as 'one of the world's greatest criminals' and write, '(Timur) has surpassed all others with reference to the murder of peaceful non-combatant Muslims and, in a much smaller degree, non-combatant non-Muslims, who were beheaded by his orders or put to death in more original ways.'

Ahmed Ibn Arabshah was a contemporary writer on Timur and wrote his work in Arabic which was translated by J.H. Sanders to English in 1936.[2] *Zafarnama,* a biography of Timur was written by Nizamuddin Shami which formed the basis of the second and more famous *Zafarnama* written by Sharafaddin Ali Yazdi around 1425. These works have a certain bias both towards and against Timur. His character notwithstanding, this chapter primarily deals with Timur's campaigns against the Jats, the infidel and idol worshippers of Turkestan[3] (post-Soviet states in Central Asia including Northern Afghanistan).

Ahmed Ibn Arabshah mentions a number of military expeditions made against the Jat country (or Turkestan) where the majority of the population were infidels and idol worshippers. However, like previous great conquerors (e.g. Mahmud Ghaznavi) they also had an army with a mixed background. Arabshah writes that the army had Turks who worshipped idols and Zoroastrians who worshipped fire. In addition to them, there were 'soothsayers, wicked enchanters and unbelievers'. He adds that idolaters carried their idols and the soothsayers spoke in verses and made no distinction between an animal that is strangled or killed with a knife.

The contemporary historians referred to Turkestan as Jattah (Jat country). In Transoxiana (the area around the Amu Darya) almost all Mongols had converted to Islam but this was not the case in Jattah. Some of their leaders had a Muslim name but the vast majority were still infidels. One of the Khans (leaders) of Jattah was Tughluq Timur Khan, son of Ughul Khan and grandson of Dawa Khan who felt it was his right to rule Transoxiana.

After the death of Tughluq Timur Khan, the Jats elected Qabl Ughlan, a descendant of Dawa Khan as their Khan.

In 1365, the Jattah forces attacked Transoxiana and were able to defeat Amir Husain and Timur in a stiff battle. They surrounded the capital Samarkand but were unable to breach the walls due to inspired defiance by the citizens. After four months of siege, the Jattah army retreated.

Meanwhile, Timur had a fallout with the Amir and even thought of forming an alliance with the Jats but as they were non-Muslims (and idol worshippers) his religious scholars encouraged reconciliation with Amir Husain. Later, Timur helped the Amir in subduing Shahs of Badakhshan (Northern Afghanistan).

Following the assassination of Husain, Timur declared himself the Amir at Balkh. During the first fifteen years of his rule, Timur led six expeditions against the Jats. In 1375, Timur encamped in Jattah country for over five months but the Jattah leader Qamruddin Dughlat kept harassing Umar Sheikh, son of Timur who was posted at Andijan (Uzbekistan). The Jats were not easily subdued. To make matters worse, Timur had to deal with the rebellion of his own officers who would defect to his opponents including the Jats

Timur's successor, Ulugh Beg (ruled 1411–49) was also a renowned mathematician and astronomer who built an observatory at Samarkand. He was defeated by Burraq Ughlan and the Jats plundered Transoxiana.

The authenticity of *Mulfuzat Timury*, the autobiography of Timur is doubted but also quoted by many historians.

The English translation of this work by Charles Stewart also makes references to the Jetes' (Jats) attack on Samarkand and numerous other campaigns against the 'infidel and idolater' Jetes by Timur.[4]

Babur on Kabul and Peshawar—Early 1500s

In 1504, Kabul came under Babur, founder of the Mughal dynasty in Hindustan (ruled 1526–30). In his memoirs, Babur claimed that Timur was his ancestor.

Babur recorded the old temple of Gor Khatri (old Peshawar) in his autobiography *Baburnama*[5]. He writes that he had heard about the place which was considered holy by the Hindu Yogis (ascetics) 'who came from long distances for pilgrimage and got their head and beards shaved'. Babur adds that once he was on his way to Bigram (present-day Peshawar) when he saw its famous ancient tree and surrounding countryside. But the guide did not take Babur to Gor Khatri due to 'its confined cells and narrow passages'. Although Babur was keen to pay a visit, he did not go as 'the day was spent'.

Babur refers to Kabul as an excellent trading centre and Hindustan's own market. He mentions that almost 8,000–10,000 horses would come to the city along with 15,000–20,000 caravans from Hindustan with household stuff, slaves, white cloth, refined sugar candy, common sugar and aromatic roots. Despite making 300–400 percent profit, many merchants were not satisfied although they would never make such profit even if they went to Cathay (Northern China) or Turkey, he noted. He adds that in Kabul, products from Khurasan, Iraq,

Turkey and China were available and Hindvi (Indian) language was spoken in the region.

Anthony Jenkinson's account—1558

In 1558, Anthony Jenkinson visited Bukhara and mentioned Indian merchants in the city. He was one of the first Europeans to explore Russia. Jenkinson writes that Bukhara was an annual resort of merchants and that great caravans from India, Persia, Balkh, Russia and other countries routinely arrived. We are told that the Indians brought doe, cotton and coarse linen to Bukhara and took away silk, red hides (for leather), horses and slaves! The Indian merchants came from as far as Bengal and regions beside the river Ganga[6].

References

1. Mohammad Habib and K.A. Nizami. (1970). *A Comprehensive History of India, Vol. 5 The Delhi Sultanate (AD 1206–1526)*. Delhi: People's Publishing.
2. J.H. Sanders (Trans.). (1936) *Tamerlane or Timur The Great Amir From the Arabic Life By Ahmed Ibn Arabshah.* London: Luzac & Co.
3. Turkestan, also spelt Turkistan (literally, 'Land of the Turks' in Persian), refers to an area in Central Asia between Siberia to the north and Tibet, India and Afghanistan to the south, the Caspian Sea to the west and the Gobi Desert to the east. The area covers a large number of countries including Russia (Tatarstan and parts of Siberia), Mongolia, the Chinese autonomous province of Xinjiang (also known as East Turkestan or Chinese Turkestan), Kazakhstan, Turkmenistan,

Tajikistan, Uzbekistan, Kyrgyzstan, and parts of Afghanistan.

4. Maj. Charles Stewart (Trans.). (1830). *Mulfuzat Timury: Autobiographical Memoirs of the Moghul Emperor Timur Written In The Jagtay Turky Language Turned Into Persian By Abu Talib Hussyny*. London: J Murray.
5. Annette S. Beveridge. (1922). *The Babur-Nama in English*. London: Luzac & Co.
6. E.D. Morgan and C.H. Coote. (1886). *Early Voyages and Travels to Russia and Persia by Anthony Jenkinson and other Englishmen*. London: Hakluyt Society.

5

Hindus in 17th Century Persia and Khurasan

Throughout the 16th, 17th and early 18th centuries, the Persian Safavid dynasty and the Mughal dynasty of India ruled among themselves different parts of the region which later came to be known as Afghanistan. Hence, almost all contemporary travellers of this period visited Isfahan and Delhi/Agra which were the capitals of the Persian and the Mughal Empires respectively. The cities of modern Afghanistan are hardly mentioned in these works. Nevertheless, there are numerous references to Hindus in Central Asia and even Turkey.

Fedot Kotov's account—1624

Fedot Kotov, the Russian, travelled to Persia, Turkey, India and to Hormuz Island in the Persian Gulf which was a great port and trade centre around 1624. Kotov lived in Isfahan which was the capital of Shah Abbas of Persia (Safavid dynasty) who held a major portion of present-day Afghanistan and the rest, especially Eastern Afghanistan was with the Mughals who ruled from Delhi (and Agra) in India. He observes that Hindu and

Muslim traders from India were doing brisk business in Persia. His account[1] is as follows:

Isfahan was the capital of Persia described as 'large and fine'. Kotov found that the citadel was poor as it was made of clay 'like the walls thrown up around gardens'. The bazaar, streets, coffee houses, hostelries and mosques were all built of stone. We are told that the storehouses had all kinds of flowers painted in many colours. Merchants from different nationalities, Tajiks, Indians, Turks, Arabs, Jews and others traded in them.

Kotov specifically mentions Multani merchants in Isfahan, some were Muslims and others believed in the sun—'when the sun begins to rise, they pray to it'. This is a reference to a sect among the Hindus who treated the sun as God. There was a very famous sun temple in Multan, which according to *The Imperial Gazetteer of India* was destroyed during the reign of Aurangzeb (1658–1707) and a Jama Masjid was erected at the site[2].

He mentions another sect of Indians who wore 'yellow paint down the forehead across the root of the nose' (*tilak*) and cremated their dead. Kotov states, 'when any one of these Indians dies they carry him outside the city and beyond the town settlement into the field and burn him on wood and scatter the ashes and they say that that man has gone to heaven and those Indians call themselves Christians'.

Kemp, who translated the Russian text clarified that Kotov confused Krishna, the Hindu God with Christ as the two words sound similar, especially in the Russian language. In the Punjabi language (including Multani), Krishna is pronounced as Krishan or simply Kishan. This may have further added to the misunderstanding.

Kotov further writes that all Indians wore clothes of white cotton and white turbans. He adds, 'In stature, they are not robust and their faces are bloodless and lean and dark.' Cotton was one of the items brought to Persia by the Indian merchants.

Kotov mentions that Kandahar used to be the Indian frontier for the Persians but Shah Abbas captured the city and made it his frontier with India. Kandahar exchanged hands between the Mughals and the Safavid dynasty several times. The Mughals made the last unsuccessful attempt to capture the city in 1653.

Adam Olearius' account—1635

Adam Olearius, a 17th century German traveller, was sent by the Duke of Holstein (the modern state of Schleswig-Holstein in north Germany) to explore trade ties with Russia. In 1635, he was sent to undertake the same venture in Persia. Later, he published a book on his travels and referred to Hindu merchants in Isfahan, capital of the Persian Empire, which included large parts of present-day Afghanistan[3].

Olearius states that merchants from all over Asia and Europe came to Isfahan and carried out both wholesale and retail trade. He adds that there were 12,000 Indian merchants in the city who sold the merchandise to shops which were nearer to their caravansaries and storehouses. The stuff sold by the Indian merchants were 'incomparably fairer and their commodities of greater value than those of Persia'. They brought musk, ambergris (both used in perfumery) and large quantities of pearls and diamonds.

Olearius observed that most of the Indian merchants had a mark of saffron upon the nose though he was unable to learn what it signified, and that they were pagans who burned the bodies of their deceased using wood from the apricot tree only. Olearius, like Kotov, mentions that they all wore cotton and the richer ones had a fine scarf with lively colours. Besides Indians, there were Turks, Jews, Armenians, Georgians, English, Dutch, French, Italian and Spaniard merchants and those from Khurasan and Bukhara among other nations.

Abbe Carre's account—1672–74

The Frenchman Abbe Carre travelled from France to India in 1672–74 through the Syrian Desert, Mesopotamia (Iraq) and the Persian Gulf. He left a detailed account of his travels in French which was later translated into English by Lady Fawcett and edited by Sir Charles Fawcett with the assistance of Sir Richard Burn in 1947.

The Frenchman refers to his stay in the house of a Hindu merchant in a village near Naband Bay in Persia. He writes, 'I was sent to the entrance of the village, to the house of a Hindu merchant who accommodated me as well as he could in the hope of a good reward'[4].

Jean Baptista Tavernier's account—1768–70

Another Frenchman, Jean Baptista Tavernier, travelled from France to Mughal India through Persia and Khurasan and left a detailed account of his travels.

Tavernier gave a route from Isfahan (Persia) to Agra (India) through Kandahar (Afghanistan). He writes that there were two routes only, either through Kabul or through Multan (Pakistan). The latter was shorter by ten days but rarely used by caravans as one had to pass through the desert and without any sight of water for three to four days. The commonly used and preferred route was through Kabul. It usually took 150 days but if merchants had urgent work they would go on horseback in parties of three or four and covered the same distance in less than half the time or in sixty to seventy-five days.

Tavernier writes that Kabul was a large town and well fortified, and that the Uzbek people came every year to sell their horses and buy sheep and other cattle. Kabul was a 'great meeting place for Tartar, Persia and India'. One could obtain wine and 'articles of food are very cheap' in Kabul. The people who inhabited the land between Kandahar and Kabul, towards the mountain of Balkh were known as Afghans and that they were 'powerful, mean and great thieves at night'!

Interestingly, Tavernier then refers to the Afghans as Indians (the northern and eastern region was then with the Mughals) and mentions their tongue-cleaning habit, 'It is the custom of these Indians to clean and scrape the tongue every morning with a small curved piece of a particular root'. The people of the subcontinent shared this hygienic habit[5].

The great trading town of Isfahan had both Jews and 'Indian idolaters' (Hindus). Tavernier writes that the Jews looked miserable and beggarly but were into all businesses and if one had to buy or sell a rich jewel than they were the people to contact. We are told that during the reign of Shah Abbas, Jews were prosecuted and 'either by force or by cunning' many were converted to Islam. Tavernier adds that 'the King (Shah Abbas) understanding that only power and fear had constrained them to turn, suffered them to resume their own religion, and to live in quiet'.

Tavernier writes that there were about 10,000–12,000 Baniyas (Hindu trading caste) in Isfahan who were identified by 'their yellow complexions, or rather by a yellow mark made with saffron upon the top of their foreheads'. Tavernier adds that 'their turbans are less than usual and their shoes are almost like ours, embroidered with flowers a-top'.

Tavernier adds that the Baniyas were all bankers and very knowledgeable about money. They controlled the money of all the powerful people and if one needed a considerable sum, they were the people to ask. If one could give good security and was ready to pay the high interest (sometimes 18 percent), the money was disbursed the very next day[6].

Evliya Çelebi's account

Mehmed Zilli (1611–82), also known as Evliya Çelebi (Çelebi is an honorific title meaning gentleman) was a native of Turkey and an explorer who travelled through the territory of the Ottoman Empire and neighbouring lands over a period of forty years. He left memoirs titled *Seyahatname* (Book of Travel) in the Turkish language. This was translated into English by Ritter Joseph Von Hammer in 1834.

Though Evliya travelled throughout the Ottoman Empire, he did not visit Khurasan. Yet he mentions the presence of Hindu fakirs in Istanbul and Indian merchants at Erzurum in Anatolia province of Turkey. He writes, 'On the outside of the windows of the court (Sultan Ahmed Mosque) there are several covered porches supported by small columns, in which, when the assembly within is too great, many of the faithful perform their devotions and the Hindu fakirs find shelter'.

He adds that Indian ships landed in Basra (Iraq), 'Euphrates and Tigris join at Kaverna and become a very large river which is ascended by Indian ships from Basra, the whole extent with all its windings is four hundred farsangs. It passes 400 towns and villages'.

In relation to the Erzurum city (Anatolia, Turkey) he writes, 'The suburb of the Georgians on the north side, is the quarter of the rich merchants; here is the custom-house where I was employed as clerk, round it are the houses of Persian, Indian, and Chinese merchants, next to the custom-houses of Constantinople and Smyrna, that of Erzerum is the most busy'.

He adds that 'the Infidels wear variegated turbans, and blue coats and the lower classes wear felt, with coarse shoes called Chark, their women wrap white sheets round their heads'[7].

Jahangir's account

The Mughal Emperor, Jahangir (1605–25) like his great-grandfather (Babur) also visited Gor Khatri (Peshawar). He mentions it in his autobiography, *Tuzuk e Jahangiri*[8], where Jahangir writes that he had encamped in the garden of Sardar Khan in the neighbourhood of Peshawar and walked round Gor Khatri. He describes it as the worshipping-place of the Yogis. He also went to meet the ascetics and obtain their grace but the Mughal ruler was left unimpressed. He states, 'But that was like looking for the phoenix or the philosopher's stone. A herd without any religious knowledge came to my view, from seeing whom I derived nothing but obscurity of mind'.

Jahangir writes that he had abolished all the transit duties in Kabul, one of the main towns on the road to Hindustan. These duties were worth 1.23 crore (12.3 million) dams. He adds that the provinces of Kabul and Kandahar rendered large sums of custom duty which was the main revenue of these provinces. Jahangir states that he remitted 'these ancient dues' which greatly benefited the people of Persia and Turan.

References

1. P.M. Kemp. (1959). *Russian Travellers to India and Persia (1624–1798)*. New Delhi: Jiwan Prakashan.
2. W.W. Hunter. (1886). *The Imperial Gazetteer of India, Vol X, Multan to Palhalli*. 2nd Ed. London: Trubner & Co.

3. Adam Olearius. (1669). *The Voyages and Travells of the Ambassadors Sent by Frederick Duke of Holstein, to the Great Duke of Muscovy and the King of Persia.* Translated from German by John Davies. 2nd Ed. London.

4. Lady Fawcett. (1947). *The Travels of Abbe Carre in India and the Near East 1672–74.* London: The Hakluyt Society.

5. V. Ball. (1889). *Travels in India by Jean Baptiste Tavernier Baron of Aubonne.* London: Macmillan.

6. J. Philips. (1678). *The Six Voyages of John Baptista Tavernier through Turky into Persia and the East Indies (Finished in the Year 1670).* London: RL & MP.

7. Ritter Joseph Von Hammer. (1834). *Narrative of Travels in Europe, Asia, and Africa, in the Seventeenth Century by Evliya Efendi.* London: William H Allen

8. Alexander Rogers (Trans.) Henry Beveridge (Ed.). (1909). *Memoirs of Jahangir.* London: Royal Asiatic Society.

6

Guru Nanak (1469–1539) and Sikhs in Afghanistan

The history of Sikhs in Khurasan starts with the founder of the Sikh religion, Guru Nanak (1469–1539) who was a prolific traveller. The life and times of the great saint is recorded in *Janamsakhis* which are semi-historical in nature as they are written in a devotional manner and do not contain dates but records of his visits to Mecca, Medina, Bagdad, Kabul and Kandahar (all in Central Asia) along with visits to Sri Lanka and within the Indian sub-continent[1]. The earliest copy belongs to the early 1600s but their further antiquity cannot be ruled out.

Guru Nanak and his companion in his travels, Bhai Mardana left Mashhad (Persia) to reach Balkh and then reached outside the city of Kabul which was under Babur at that time. In one instance, the Guru met some holy men who enquired what brought a Hindu ascetic to a land of Muslims. The Guru replied that 'the Almighty created the same Divine Light, that pervades all. God has created all beings in the same mould. However, some of them wear *janeu* while some others got themselves circumcised'. The holy men were very impressed with the Guru. The Guru stayed in the city for some time and then travelled further in the country[2].

They also went to meet Maan Chand, son of Khan Chand who lived in Kabul city. The Guru sent for him through a local Pathan. Maan Chand met Guru Nanak and later became his follower and a preacher of Guru's doctrine in this region[3].

The *Janamsakhi* records that in Sultanpur (about 8 km from Jalalabad) a shepherd boy while grazing his goats got really thirsty and fell on the ground. Both Guru Nanak and his companion Bhai Bala were there and the Guru asked Bhai Bala to get some water. The latter answered that there was no water nearby, the Guru then asked him to lift a rock and when Bala lifted one, a stream of water came out. The stream still exists and is famous as 'Tohri Bala'[4], a famous place in relation to Guru Nanak and the Sikhs in Afghanistan. The place finds mention even in Charles Masson's travel account written in the 1840s.

Guru Nanak and Bhai Mardana came to Ar Randha (Arghandab) river and met a Mughal Pathan fakir who introduced himself as Yaar Ali and asked about Guru Nanak. The Guru said he was a *Banda* of *Khuda,* a servant of God. The Fakir then asked who his *Peer* (spiritual teacher) was. The Guru replied that the one who had created this world was his *Peer* and the fakir fell at the feet of the Guru.

At the time of Guru Nanak, the route through Kurram Pass was commonly used for the journey from Kabul to Peshawar. Guru Nanak also took this route[5]. There are Gurdwaras in Kurram Agency in FATA (Federal Administered Territory Area) which is now a part of the Khyber Pakhtunkhwa province in Pakistan bordering Afghanistan.

Babur Vani is the name given to the four hymns of Guru Nanak in the Guru Granth Sahib (compiled in 1605) referring to the invasion of Hindustan by Babur and the devastation caused by the Mughals. In his autobiography, Babur notes that those towns or areas who submitted to him were spared but those who chose to defend their towns, there even the innocent civilians were not spared. Babur defeated and replaced the Pathan Lodi dynasty (1451–1526) that ruled parts of Northern Hindustan.

The Guru Granth Sahib has spiritual poetic compositions in the Gurmukhi script from the first five Sikh Gurus and the ninth one along with compositions of Hindu, Sikh and Muslim saints. It is considered as the living Guru by the Sikhs. Below are a few lines from three *shabads* (compositions) of *Babur Vani*[6]:

> *Having conquered Khurasan, Babar has terrified Hindustan.*
>
> *The creator takes not the blame on Himself and has sent the Mughal as death's myrmidon.*
>
> *So much beating was inflicted that people shrieked. Does not Thou O God, feel compassion?*
>
> *O maker, art the equal master of all.*
>
> (GGS, p. 360)
>
> *When Babar's rule was proclaimed, then no (Pathan) prince ate his food.*
>
> *Some lost their five times of prayer, and of some, the time of worship is gone.*
>
> (GGS, p. 417)

Bringing the marriage party of sin, Babar has hastened from Kabul and demands perforce the gift of our Land, etc. O Lalo.

Modesty and righteousness both have vanished, and falsehood moves about as the leader, O Lalo.

(GGS, p. 722)

Sikh Gurus and their followers in Kabul

The Mughal Emperor Babur captured Kabul in 1504 and by 1526 he was the master of North India. Kabul became one of the provinces of Hindustan (contemporary writers use this name). Indian merchants had been regularly visiting Kabul throughout the centuries. As mentioned earlier, Babur referred to Kabul as Hindustan's own market. The province of Kabul remained with Hindustan until 1738 when it was conquered by Nadir Shah, the Persian ruler. During this period, the Sikh chroniclers record a number of names and instances when Sikh followers in Kabul came to the region now known as East Punjab, to pay respects to the Sikh Gurus.

Sarup Das Bhalla, who was a descendant of Guru Amar Das (1552–74), the third Sikh Guru, wrote *Mahima Prakash* in 1776. This manuscript mentions the name of *Kabul wali Mai* (Lady from Kabul) who did *seva* (voluntary service) with great devotion when the digging of the *Baoli* (stepwell) at Goindawal (district Tarn Taran, East Punjab) was undertaken by the third Guru. The manuscript refers to Bibi (sister) Bhago who was in-charge of the *Manji* (Sikh preaching centre) in Kabul while according to an inscription in Gurdwara Haveli Sahib in Goindwal her name was Mai Sevan.

These may be two different women or the same individual but it is remarkable that there was a Sikh woman preacher in the 16th century.

Prof. Ganda Singh writes that Baba Ganj Baksh from Gurdaspur was an important Udasi Sadhu who became a Sikh during the time of Guru Amardas and started preaching. His followers are known as Ganj Bakshiye. A Gurdwara was named after him in Kabul. It cannot be verified if he came to Kabul or the Gurdwara was built by one of his followers[7].

Guru Arjan (1581–1606) was the fifth Guru of the Sikhs. His cousin, Bhai Gurdas wrote *Vaaran* which is much revered by the Sikhs and it mentions the name of Bhai Rekh Rao and Bhai Bhana Mallan, the Sikh residents of Kabul. The manuscript *Sikhan di Bhagat Mala* written by Bhai Mani Singh around 1720s elaborates that they looked after the stores of the local chief. A complaint was made against them that they were using short weights and misappropriated the provisions in the stores. However, their devotion and piousness proved their honesty. The weights were tested and found to be correct. Some Sikh chroniclers have mentioned the same anecdote but for Bhai Katara.

The Gurdwara Pipali Sahib situated a mile and a half north-west of Harmandar Sahib (also known as the Golden Temple) in Amritsar commemorates the visit of Guru Arjan when he reached here to greet the *Sangat* (Sikhs) of Kabul who had come to participate in the digging of tanks. The Guru built four water tanks in Amritsar city. The site was also visited by the Guru Hargobind[8].

Guru Hargobind (1606–44) was the sixth Guru of the Sikhs. Following the execution of the fifth Guru (considered as martyrdom by the Sikhs) on the orders of Mughal Emperor Jahangir, Guru Hargobind armed the Sikhs and started the martial tradition among them.

The manuscript *Gurbilas Padshahi Chhevee,* a biographical account of the sixth Guru written in the first quarter of the 18th century records the name of Bhai Karori, a Sikh horse dealer in Kabul who sent two of his finest horses Dilbagh and Gulbagh as an offering to the Guru. Shortly after, Bhai Tara Chand and Bakht Mall who were *Masands* (Sikh preachers) in Kabul travelled with the *Sangat* and the horses to meet the Guru at Kiratpur, East Punjab. On the way, the horses were forcibly taken by the *Faujdar* (Garrison Commander) of Lahore. The Sikhs informed Guru Hargobind of the highhandedness of the *Faujdar* when Bidhi Chand, a Sikh was able to recover the horses through a stratagem.

An early 17th-century Persian manuscript *Dabistan-i-Mazahib* written by Zulfiqar Ardastani has a chapter on *Nanakpanthis* (followers of Guru Nanak). It mentions two anecdotes relating to Bhai Sadh who lived near Balkh. The anecdotes show that a devoted Sikh is contented with the will of the Almighty which may bring joys and sorrows in life and their devotion to the Guru.

On Guru's order, Bhai Sadh left Balkh for Iraq to buy horses. Shortly after, his son fell sick and he was asked by his companions to go back to his son. He replied that if his son perished, it was the will of the God and that there were enough resources in the house to cremate him. Bhai Sadh added that he would return only after fulfilling the mission. Though the son passed away, the father did not return mid-way.

In the second incident, Ardastani was travelling with Sadh from Kabul to Punjab when the former discovered that the belt of his sheepskin had snapped. Sadh immediately took off his *zannar* (the sacred thread) and made a joint there. Ardastani was surprised and asked what he had done. Sadh replied, 'The wearing of the sacred thread is an undertaking of service. Whenever I neglect the service of my guests and friends, I become a non-wearer of it'. And Bhai Sadh quoted a verse, 'This knotless relation, though slender as a single strand, is rosary in a cloister and a *zannar* in a temple'[9].

Bhai Sabhaga, a Sikh from Peshawar, brought five horses from Kabul as an offering to Guru Hargobind in the latter's court at Hargobindpur. *Mahan Kosh* quotes *Suraj Prakash Granth* that *'Dhani bado aru nam sabhaga'* (Sabhaga was rich in money and virtues).

The 18th century manuscript, *Mahima Prakash* mentions that Bhai Gonda was sent to Kabul to preach the Sikh doctrine by the seventh Guru, Har Rai (1644–61). He established a *Dharamsaal* (earlier name of Gurdwara) over there. The manuscript also records an anecdote about his devotion.

Guru Tegh Bahadur (1664–75) was the ninth Guru of the Sikhs. He was executed (considered martyred by the Sikhs) by the Mughal Emperor Aurangzeb. The near contemporary Persian sources like *Khulasat-ut-Tawarikh,*

Nuskha-i Dilkusha and *Ibratnama* makes mention of this extraordinary event in Sikh history as it eventually led to the establishment of the Khalsa order.

Giani Gian Singh mentions that Guru Tegh Bahadur was travelling towards Samao (Bathinda, East Punjab) when he was informed of the *Sangat* from Kabul and Peshawar coming to see him. The Guru halted at Samoa and sat under a tree to receive the *Sangat*. When the *Sangat* arrived, a farmer working in the nearby fields provided bread and buttermilk for them. The Guru blessed the peasant and a Gurdwara was built to commemorate this event[10].

The last and tenth Guru of the Sikhs, Guru Gobind Singh led the Sikhs from 1675–1708. Before his final departure, he bestowed Guruship upon the Adi Granth, the religious book of Sikhs and named it Guru Granth Sahib.

Prof. Hari Ram Gupta quotes from contemporary records that a Duni Chand from Kabul bought a costly tent at Anandpur (East Punjab) to be used for Guru Gobind Das (later, Guru Gobind Singh from 1699) for holding durbar in 1688–89. The tent was made of the finest silk and had numerous pictures stitched with threads of gold and strings of pearls hung around it. The flooring had beautiful Persian carpets. The gesture touched the pride of Pahari Rajput ruler Bhim Chand who already held a grudge against the Guru which later led to the Battle of Bhangani (1689), first of the several battles between the Sikhs and the Pahari Rajput rulers.

Bhai Nand Lal (1633–1715), a great poet and scholar of Persia was born in Ghazni and was one of the poets in the court of Guru Gobind Singh. His compositions written under the penname Goya is much revered and sung by the Sikhs. His father was Diwan Chhajju Ram, Mir Munshi or chief secretary of the Governor of Ghazni.

At the age of nineteen Nand Lal migrated to Multan which was a big city of merchants. He settled in Multan and took a local Sikh woman as his wife. He got employed by the local chief and was soon appointed as Mir Munshi. It is through his wife that Nand Lal became close to the Sikh doctrine and the socio-political circumstances that led him to seek refuge under Guru Gobind Singh at Anandpur. His life and work have been covered in detail by Prof. Ganda Singh[11].

Sadly, the Sikhs in general and particularly those from Afghanistan did not share his remarkable work with fellow Afghans. Only a small part of his devotional poetry written in praise of Guru Gobind Singh is sung by the Sikhs as most of his poetic compositions are in Persian, a language alien to most present-day Sikhs.

Early Sikhs of 17th century

The 17th century Persian manuscript *Dabistan-i-Mazahib* provides an early account of Sikhs. Initially, it was attributed to Kashmiri writer Muhsin Fani but now most historians agree that it was written by Mir Zulfiqar Ardestani (d.1670), a Zoroastrian priest from Persia who travelled and stayed in Hindustan for many years. This is a well-known account as it makes reference to the *Deen-e-Elahi*, a 'religion' started by Akbar the Great, the Mughal ruler of Hindustan.

The manuscript was first translated by David Shea and Anthony Troyer in 1843. Prof. Ganda Singh translated the chapter on Sikhs titled *Nanakpanthis* in 1930. *Panth* means path hence, *Nanakpanthis* refer to the followers of (Guru) Nanak. The chapter on *Nanakpanthis* is not without errors but provides a neutral account and the author states that he personally knew the sixth and seventh Sikh Gurus namely Guru Hargobind and Guru Har Rai. The work refers to a *Nanakpanthi* named Sadh who lived near Sadh and his journeys to Iraq, Kabul and Punjab[12].

In relation to the religious practice, Ardestani writes that the *Nanakpanthis* condemned idol worship and 'do not read mantras of the Hindus'. They did not venerate their temples of idols, nor did they esteem their Avatars (like the famous incarnations of Lord Vishnu). The *Nanakpanthis* had no regard for the Sanskrit language which according to the Hindus was the 'speech of the angels'.

The manuscript mentions that during Guru Arjan's time, the number of *Nanakpanthis* increased and 'there were not many cities in the inhabited countries' where some of them were not to be found. The majority of the *Masands* (preachers nominated in an area) were Jats (the farmer caste) although the Gurus are Khatris (Punjabi variant of Kshatriya, the second caste). There is though, no restriction based on caste.

Ardestani mentions the number of defensive battles Guru Hargobind had fought against the imperial Mughal regime. He states that the Guru had seven hundred horses in his stables and 'three hundred cavaliers and sixty artillerymen were always in his service'. He describes the Guru as a monotheist and a 'Unitarian' and states, 'The world is a baseless manifestation and a bodiless appearance. Its reality is God Most High'.

The concept of *Sangat* (Sikh congregation) and *Ardas* is explained. Ardestani writes that they 'join their hands in prayers towards the Guru and pray that his wish is fulfilled'. He adds that 'The Guru, too requests his wishes to be fulfilled in the same manner from the *Sangat*'.

Ardestani records two anecdotes regarding Sadh, a devoted *Nanakpanthi* who lived near Balkh. Sadh is described as a 'person who does not become elated by joys and depressed by sorrows'.

Sikhs and Afghans (1748–1849)

Ahmed Shah Abdali's first invasion to North India was in 1748 which was met with failure. Sardar Ala Singh, founder of erstwhile Patiala state, was part of the Mughal forces which repulsed the Afghans[13] but within a decade Abdali was able to annex Punjab. The next 101 years the Afghan and the Sikh ruling elite were neighbours and mostly antagonists.

Abdali, the founder of modern Afghanistan led almost nine invasions of North India till 1767. During this period, his looting expedition came to such a stage that people of Punjab came up with a proverb, *Khada peeta lahe da, baki Ahmed Shahe da*. It means, eat and drink what you can, the rest (anything saved) belongs to (will be taken by) Ahmed Shah.

The Sikh Confederacy known as *Misls* defended Punjab using guerrilla warfare. To teach Sikhs a lesson, Abdali and his Lahore governor ransacked and flattened the Harmandar Sahib (Golden Temple) at Amritsar. In 1764, within a single day, Abdali killed more than 20,000 Sikhs including women and children. However, the very next year the Sikhs were able to capture Punjab, the territory from Indus to Yamuna. The city of Multan and neighbouring areas remained under the Sikh *Misl* Sardars (leaders) for a decade before passing on to the Afghans. Timur, the successor to Ahmed Shah was unable to re-capture Punjab but was successful in Multan in 1779[14].

Shah Shuja Durrani, the grandson of Ahmed Shah, was deposed from the throne in 1809. He spent some time in Lahore under Maharaja Ranjit Singh and later in Ludhiana in Punjab, under the British. In 1837, the Persians with Russian support laid siege on Herat. The British had to send their fleet to the Persian Gulf in preparation. This convinced the British to have a friendly regime in Afghanistan as it was felt that Russia could attack India. Amir Dost Mohammed Khan was happy to be neutral, although reluctant to have a permanent British ambassador in Kabul and unwilling to forsake his claim of Peshawar as well (which was with Ranjit Singh).

In 1838, Shah Shuja was able to secure support from the British East India Company and Maharaja Ranjit Singh, the Sikh ruler of Lahore, who was the neighbour of the Afghan state. It was agreed that Shah Shuja would be re-instated as the Amir of Afghanistan and Dost Mohammed would be removed.

Maharaja Ranjit Singh (1799–1839) had successfully annexed Kashmir, Multan, Attock, Dejarat, Hazara and Peshawar which were all under the Afghans. However, the loss of Peshawar was the most hurtful for the Afghans and ever since his first victory in the city in 1818, the Maharaja had to constantly defend the region from the Afghan and local adversaries. Although he was successful in most of these campaigns, if not all, due to a superior and modernised army still it kept him busy. It made sense to have a friendly regime at Kabul hence, one of the clauses was that Shah Shuja would forfeit any claim on Peshawar in lieu of the Sikh support. Shah Shuja was re-instated as Amir of Afghanistan in 1839, almost thirty years after he was initially deposed by his brother. However, Shah Shuja was murdered in 1842 and the British who were already fed up with the costly (human and monetary) war which later came to be known as First Anglo-Afghan war invited Dost Mohammad Khan who was earlier deposed by the British to take up the reign in Afghanistan.

Khushwant Singh writes that the new Sikh ruler, Maharaja Sher Singh was unhappy and felt that the British had used Sikhs in the Afghanistan campaign to their own benefit. Apparently, the British forgot to consult the successor of Ranjit Singh regarding the reinstatement of the old adversary of the Sikhs, Dost Mohammed Khan to head the helm of affairs in Afghanistan. When Dost Mohammed passed through Lahore on his way to Kabul, the Sikh ruler gave him a huge welcome and expensive gifts[15]. The Khan was also inclined to form better relations with Sikhs as they were neighbours. A few months later Sher Singh was murdered which eventually led to the British occupation of Punjab.

In 1848–49, the Sikhs fought the British which came to be known as the Second Anglo-Sikh War. Dost Mohammed was sympathetic to the Sikh cause and sent irregular Afghan mercenaries which fought alongside the Sikhs in the Battle of Gujrat in February 1849. The superior artillery of the British won the day and this ended the era of Sikh and Afghan relationships on a rare co-operation.

Masson refers to the interesting friendship between Amir Dost Mohammad and the Sikh chief Jai Singh Attariwala who was sent on a mission to Peshawar in 1820 where he met the Amir. Masson writes, 'An endless succession of feasts and entertainments, of riotous debauches and nautches, in the Bagh Nura Khaka, testified to the friendship between the old Sikh chieftain and the youthful Durrani'[16].

Harbans Singh in *Encyclopaedia of Sikhism* notes that fearing chastisement from the Maharaja (Ranjit Singh), Jai Singh plotted to kill the king along with two others. The plot failed and Jai Singh fled to Peshawar and then to his friend Dost Mohammed. Later, when the Afghan and the Sikh armies met on occasional skirmishes, Masson notes, 'One day, some thirty Sikh heads were brought in and affixed to the house of Jai Singh. He accepted the act as a warning to decamp, and fled to the Sikh army'.

Harbans Singh notes that during the campaign of Peshawar in 1823, Jai Singh returned to the Maharaja who forgave him and later deputed him as one of the agents to arrange for a meeting with Yar Mohammed and Dost Mohammed Khan. Jai Singh died in 1838[17].

The *Misl* period and Maharaja Ranjit Singh's reign have been discussed in much detail by Prof. Hari Ram Gupta in his famous work, *The History of the Sikhs* in five volumes. A short summary of the Sikh-Afghan relationship during this period has been given an overview as further details fall outside the preview of this book.

References

1. Prof. Kirpal Singh in 1969 wrote a monumental work, *Janamsakhi Parampara* in the Punjabi language. He compared all the *Janamsakhis* and *Vaaran* (verses) of Bhai Gurdas and using analytical and modern historical tools provided pieces of evidence to the travels and lifetime of Guru Nanak.
2. *Janamsakhi* Bhai Mani Singh, also known as *Sikhan di Bhagat Mala* and *Gyan Ratnawali.*
3. *Janamsakhi* Bhai Bala.
4. *Janamsakhi* Bhai Bala.

5. Kirpal Singh. (1969). *Janamsakhi Parampara*. Patiala: Punjabi University.
6. Translation of Guru Granth Sahib by Manmohan Singh.
7. See chapter titled 'Gurdwaras of Afghanistan'.
8. Kahn Singh Nabha. (1930). *Gur Shabad Ratna Mahan Kosh*.
9. Ganda Singh. (1967). *Nanak Panthis or The Sikh and Sikhism of the 17th Century in The Panjab Past and Present*. Patiala: Punjabi University.
10. Harbans Singh. (1992–98). *Encyclopaedia of Sikhism*. Patiala: Punjabi University.
11. Ganda Singh. (1968). *Bhai Nand Lal Granthavali*. Patiala: Punjabi University.
12. Ganda Singh. (1967). *Nanak Panthis or The Sikh and Sikhism of the 17th Century in The Panjab Past and Present*. Patiala: Punjabi University.
13. *Tarikh-e Ahmad Shahi,* in H.R. Gupta. Hari Ram Gupta. (1979). *The History of the Sikhs, Vol 3*. 2nd Ed. New Delhi: Munshiram Manoharlal Publishers.
14. Maj. J. Browne. (1788). 'An History of the Origin and Progress of the Sikhs'. *Early European Accounts of the Sikhs,* by Ganda Singh (1962). Calcutta: Firma.
15. Khushwant Singh. (1966). *History of the Sikhs, Vol 2*. New Delhi: Oxford University Press.
16. Charles Masson. (1844). *Narrative of Various Journeys in Balochistan, Afghanistan, the Panjab and Kalat*. London: Richard Bentley.
17. Harbans Singh. (1992–98). *Encyclopaedia of Sikhism*. Patiala: Punjabi University.

7

Hindus in 18th Century Persia and Khurasan

Jonas Hanway's account

Jonas Hanway (1712–86) was an English traveller and merchant who came to Persia in December 1743 and recorded the last years of Nadir Shah (1688–1747) who reigned from 1736 until his assassination in 1747. His vast empire included the Khurasan among many countries in Central Asia.

Hanway was sent to Persia and Russia to assess the trade ties and investigate the English agent John Elton who had established trade in the region in 1740. Elton was building a fleet for Nadir Shah in the Caspian Sea and was able to secure trading privileges from the ruler. But the Russians took a negative view of it, especially Elton's role as a 'Persian naval commander' and a merchant. They dubbed him a spy and smuggler which necessitated the visit of Hanway to the region for 'damage control'.

When Hanway went back to England in 1750, he published *An Historical Account of the British Trade over the Caspian Sea* in four volumes. Hanway mentions his meeting with the Hindu merchants and carpenters, and visiting their places of worship among other things. Hanway does not mention the word Hindu but instead refers to them as 'Indian pagans' and talks about their idol worship. One can safely conclude that he is referring to Hindus.

Hanway writes that Astrakhan (Southern Russia) was a big and famous city, about sixty miles from the Caspian Sea, situated in the delta of the river Volga. The city was named after Hajji Tarkhan, a Tartar (Turkic speaking people living in Russia and post-Soviet republics, also referred as Turco-Mongol people) who founded it. The Czar of Russia (Emperor) captured it in 1554 and again in 1668. The Czar used a large number of 'flat bottom vessels' to bring his troops from Kazan city. Hanway states that there were 70,000 inhabitants; the majority were Armenians and Tartars of various denominations, with a few Persians and Indians (Hindus). Hanway observes that the 'manners and customs' of the population was 'an epitome of Asia'.

Hanway adds that the soil was extremely fertile and fruit was in abundance. However, their 'immoderate use' had made the people temperamental! The water-melons were reputed for their flavour, colour and 'taste much the same as in Portugal'. We are told that this very juicy fruit grew best in the sand.

Hanway writes that his curiosity took him to the small Hindu temple to see the 'devotion of the Indian pagans'. The priest used 'beads, incense, caps, prostrations and offerings'. The temple had 'aloft small bells' with other music, and sang with 'utmost devotion'.

Hanway was not impressed with the idol worship and writes that the idol was 'ugly and deformed to a degree of horror'. He was offered some fruits which were presented to the idol but Hanway declined. His dislike is evident when he states he refused 'not without melancholy reflections on the abject state to which human reason is frequently reduced'.

The local population (Tartars) by faith were totally against 'image worship' and did not ever carry coins which had an engraving of man, bird, beast, creeping thing, or insect, into their places of worship. Hanway added that their 'devotion is in silence and prostrations'.

Elton found good timber in Gilan and neighbouring provinces but roads were bad which made it impractical to transport them to the shipyard (near the Caspian Sea). The province of Mazandaran provided iron ore but there was no one who could cast the anchor. Elton found Russian anchors that were lost over the years on the coast. There was a great need of carpenters and Elton 'collected a few Indians', Russian renegades and one English ship carpenter whom Elton had encouraged to leave his ship.

The Persians had 'very little maritime strength' and had twenty to thirty ships in the Caspian Sea partly built in Europe, some in Pegu (Bago, a coastal city in Burma) and Surat (in India). The ships were navigated by Indians and Portuguese. Hanway slightly contradicts himself here and states that most of the ship-carpenters on the Caspian Sea were Indian 'who performed their business with delicacy'. Hanway adds that they were slow, unfit for large work as Indians did not have much understanding of the structure of vessels and method of navigating the ships.

Interestingly, Hanway mentions that there were a considerable number of Persians settled in India especially in the trading towns of Malabar and Coromandel coasts. There were some who had taken refuge in the northern and western parts of India as well.

In relation to Bukhara, Hanway writes that Nadir Shah captured Bukhara and the state lost its 'silver money'. The Persian and Indian silver coin was used during this period.

Hanway describes Mashhad as the capital of Khurasan and the favourite city of Nadir Shah which was governed by his son. The city was situated to the north of a 'ridge of mountains' and 'well supplied with water'. During peacetime, Mashhad was a place of great trade and caravans would come daily from Bukhara (now in Uzbekistan), Balkh, Badakhshan, Kandahar (all in Afghanistan), India and all parts of Persia. The markets were large and well built 'filled with rich merchandise' and visited by people of different nations. There were about ninety caravanserais, all in a good state of repair in the city. We are told that no less than 15,000 men were killed in the province and neighbouring areas when there was a rebellion in 1743. Previously, many Indian and Armenian merchants lived here along with the Tartars.

Hanway writes 250 batmans (mounds) of indigo from Lahore was brought by the Indians who were around in considerable numbers and they also traded in cloth from Rasht (near the Caspian Sea in Iran).

Hanway mentions the famous fire temple Ateshgah at Baku (now in Azerbaijan). He writes that there was a small temple where presently the Indians worshipped (previously someone else?) with a three feet tall altar whence a blue flame came out of a hollow cane. The colour was gentle and purer than the lamp. The Hindus believed the flame continued since the great flood (time immemorial) and would last till the 'end of the world'[1].

Hanway adds that there were normally about forty to fifty devotees that came on pilgrimage from their own country and lived on herbs and roots found nearby.

According to Hanway, Shamikie was the capital of Shirvan province which is now in Azerbaijan. Hanway mentions that the shops of the Armenians, Georgians, Indians, Tartars and even the Persian citizens were either locked up or plundered by the Persian army. Hanway could not find the reason behind the 'insolence, inhumanity, and rapaciousness of the soldiers'.

The Kerman city in Persia shared the name of the province and was famous for its wools. This wool which came from the neighbouring mountain sheep and was of the best quality drew a lot of merchants (including Hindu) to the city. Indian merchants were also settled in Isfahan.

Mahmud Hotak, the ruler of Persia from 1722–25, had an Indian governor from Kabul. Hanway in his book has mentioned Indian Muslims specifically hence here he is referring to a Hindu. Mahmud raised this man to the office of 'high priest' next only to Amanullah, the richest man in his court. The 'greater part' of the success of Mahmud in battles was attributed to this man's sorcery! Mahmud would not do anything without his advice and would advance half-way to meet him. Mahmud would kiss his hands and take his place only after this Indian (Hindu) was seated! When Mahmud died, either of illness or was murdered, the fortunes of 'Mi-Angi' the Hindu governor went downhill. Mahmud's cousin, Ashraf Hotak who became the new ruler confiscated his estate and exiled him to Kandahar with enough money to spend the rest of his life 'in ease and quiet'.

George Forster's account

George Forster (1752–91) was a traveller, writer and civil servant of the East India Company. He travelled from Bengal to England in 1782–83 in the disguise of a Muslim merchant. His knowledge of Persian and Hindustani languages along with the Hindu religion came in handy during his visit to Afghanistan. He writes about Hindus in the country in some detail and many of them helped him. His memoir, *A Journey from Bengal to England, through the Northern Part of India, Kashmir, Afghanistan, and Persia, and into Russia, by the Caspian Sea:* Volume 1, was published in 1790 and the second volume was published in 1798 after his death.

Forster writes that the modern city of Peshawar was founded by the Mughal Emperor Akbar (1556–1605) and since 'the Afghans were averse from dwelling in towns and the occupations of commerce' he encouraged the inhabitants of Punjab, both Hindus and Muslims to settle in the city.

Forster mentions a helpful Hindu who pleaded on his behalf to the Afghans who were harassing him at Dickah, a small village on the southern bank of the Kabul River. This Hindu used his good offices to negotiate and pay a small ransom to have the English traveller released but not before getting a blow on his face from the Afghan adversaries. Forster was so grateful for this Hindu's perseverance that he writes, 'this generous Hindoo, who, l hope, will undergo no further transmigration'.

Forster travelled in Afghanistan during the reign of Timur Shah Durrani (1772–93), son of Ahmed Shah, the founder of modern Afghanistan. Timur Shah is best remembered for transferring the capital from Kandahar to Kabul. The Sikh Confederacy known as *Misls* were able to capture Punjab, the territory from Indus to Yamuna rivers in 1765 during Ahmed Shah's reign. Timur was unable to re-capture Punjab but was successful in Multan in 1779–80. The city remained under the Sikh *Misl* Sardars for a decade before passing on to the Afghans.

Forster states that the Hindus of Kabul were ensured of 'security of person and property' as one of their own sect members (another Hindu) controlled the revenue of the Shah and was favoured by him. The traveller mentioned Jews in the city who were held in abhorrence by the Muslims but according to Forster, it was due to the 'close commercial' rivalry.

The Shah at Kabul maintained a close contact (probably due to trade) with Balkh. The great bazaar in the city was crowded with Uzbeks who had similar facial features as the 'Chinese and Malays but harsher'. Many foreign communities visited the city and the Hindus mainly from Peshawar contributed to the business by their 'superior industry and knowledge of commerce'. Foster compares that the Hindus enjoyed almost the same (if not less) liberty and protection in Balkh as they experienced in India.

Forster states that the town of Ghazni stood on a hill and at the foot ran a small river and the town's borders were surrounded by some fruit gardens. There were some Hindu families and a few Muslims in this small town.

The city of Kandahar had many Hindu families mainly from Multan and Rajput (Rajasthan?) districts and that by their handwork and mercantile knowledge had increased the trade and wealth of the city. A large number of shops were occupied by these Hindus and they enjoyed liberty and protection from the authorities.

Forster found two caravansaries in Herat with about one hundred Hindu merchants mainly from Multan who were doing brisk business and giving a long chain of credits. They were 'valuable subjects of the government'. He further states that due to the 'oppressive treatment' by the Persians, these merchants rarely brought their women to that region.

Forster states that when the Hindus crossed Attock (the last city of Hindustan) they wore long cloth coats and high caps (the local dress). Some Jewish merchants also resided in Herat and as they and the Armenians were conversant with the local language, they had little problem in mixing with the local Muslim society.

About a hundred Hindu families from Multan and Jaisalmer (border town of Rajasthan) were settled in Herat and occupied quarters in which no Muslim was permitted to reside. Forster expresses his surprise that the Brahmins among these Hindus were known by the title of *Peerzadah* (literally, the son of *Peer*, in practice, it would be used for descendants as well). The English traveller has not given any details on this appellation.

Forster writes that 'small companies' of Hindus were settled in the Persian cities of Mashhad, Yazd, Kashan, Qazvin and some parts of the Caspian Sea (Shore). More extensive Hindu societies were found in different towns of the Persian Gulf who did 'valuable commerce' with the western coast of India (most probably Sindh).

Baku is the capital and largest city of Azerbaijan now. Forster states that a society of Hindus from Multan had long been established in Baku. They along with Armenians were the main merchants in Shirvan (another major city of Azerbaijan). Silk and saffron were the main items of trade. In addition to Hindu merchants, it was visited by sadhus (ascetics) as well.

Forster had visited the famous Fire Temple, 'Ateshgah' in Baku. Forster mentions that the temple fire was used for cooking as well as to provide warmth in the winter season. The temple is now a museum which has inscriptions in Sanskrit, Persian and Punjabi (Gurmukhi) scripts which states that it was (re)built in 1745.

He writes, 'This religious retirement, where the devotees worship their deity in the semblance of fire, is a square of about thirty yards, surrounded with a low wall, and contains many apartments; in each of which is a small volcano of sulphurous fire, issuing from the ground through a furnace, or funnel, constructed in the form of a Hindoo altar'.

Forster writes that the Multani Hindus in Baku were going to Astrakhan (Southern Russia). The city had a population of about eight thousand including a 'small society' of Hindus. The Hindus enjoyed 'very fair indulgence' and performed their rituals and worship with freedom. They were a mercantile class and not permanent residents of the city and did not bring their females to the region. Forster laments that the Hindus at Astrakhan had kept no record of their first settlement.

The Hindus and even the Sikhs were well settled in Afghanistan not only in the main cities but even in small towns and villages. Some had settled in the country for long and had families but there were many Hindu merchants from Sindh and Rajputana (modern Rajasthan) who traded in the country. This mercantile community came alone having left their womenfolk in their native provinces. According to George Forster, the Mughal ruler Akbar (1556–1605) built modern Peshawar and brought Hindus to the city.

John Griffiths' Memorandum, 1794

Another account comes from John Griffiths, who was an employee of the East India Company and a resident at Basra factory in Iraq for some time and then served as the chief of the Surat factory in India. During his stay in Surat, Griffiths wrote a letter to Alexander Adamson at Bombay giving him information regarding the character of the inhabitants on the banks of the Indus, the dominion of the Sikhs in Punjab and of the Durranis in south-eastern Afghanistan.

Prof. Ganda Singh included this Memorandum in his book, *Early European Accounts of the Sikhs* under the chapter titled 'A Memorandum on the Panjab and Kandahar from Mr (John) Griffiths to Alexander Adamson dated Surat, 17th February 1794'. Under the dominion of Durranis, Griffiths gives very interesting information, he writes that the principal inhabitants were Muslims, with some Hindus, who had adopted the 'institutions of Baba Nanak'. Griffiths erroneously writes that they 'are called Kratri' unless he meant 'Khatris'. In essence, he was stating that some Hindus had adopted the religion of Guru Nanak and became Sikhs. Most of the Afghan Sikhs and the Hindus belonged to the Khatri (or Arora) caste that followed the mercantile or trader profession.

This is the first European reference to Sikhs in Afghanistan. Rather than Hindus, it would have been *Sahajdhari* Sikhs (with shaven hair) who would have taken *Khande di Pahul* and become Khalsa Sikhs. Richard Burton explored the religious practices of Sindhi Hindus and found they also followed the 'faith of Nanak Shah' and recited compositions and hymns from the Guru Granth Sahib. However, none of the British travellers, explorers and spies tried to 'scratch the surface' and find out more about the faith of the Afghan Hindus. It would have been difficult to facially distinguish a Hindu from a *Sahajdhari* unless probed. A Khalsa Sikh with his 5Ks and turban would have stood out, unlike a *Sahajdhari* or a Hindu. The Afghan Hindus and to a slightly lesser extent the Sikhs have not kept any record of themselves which further adds to the problem.

References

1. Jonas Hanway. (1753). *An Historical Account of the British Trade over the Caspian Sea: With a Journal of Travels from London Through Russia Into Persia; and Back Through Russia, Germany and Holland. To which are Added, the Revolutions of Persia During the Present Century, with the Particular History of the Great Usurper Nadir Kouli. In Four Volumes*. London.
2. George Forster. (1790). *A Journey from Bengal to England, Through the Northern Part of India, Kashmir, Afghanistan, and Persia, and into Russia, by the Caspian Sea*. London.
3. Ganda Singh. (1962). *Early European Accounts of the Sikhs*, Calcutta: Firma K.L. (Satnam Singh from Denmark brought this account to the author's attention).
4. Richard Burton. (1851). *Sindh and the Races that Inhabit the Valley of the Indus with Notices of the Topography and History of the Province*. London: W.M.H. Allen.

8

Afghan Hindus and Sikhs in Early 19th Century

Mountstuart Elphinstone's account

In 1808, Mountstuart Elphinstone[1] was sent to Afghanistan by the British to study and possibly make an alliance lest the Russians decided to invade the sub-continent. Kabul and Peshawar were a part of Mughal Hindustan from the 1520s until 1738. Then it passed on to Nadir Shah, the Persian ruler and then to Ahmed Shah Durrani in 1748. Peshawar was lost to Maharaja Ranjit Singh in 1818. Till date, no Pathan from either side of the Durand Line would argue that it was not a part of the greater Pashtun region.

Elphinstone writes that the Afghans (majority of whom were Sunnis) considered the Shias more infidel than a Hindu and had a great aversion for the Persian religion (Shia majority country) probably due to the 'injuries' the country suffered at their hands. A large part of Afghanistan, especially the Southern part remained with the Persians while the Northern part remained with the Mughals. Unlike George Forster, Elphinstone mentions Sikhs (in Afghanistan) numerous times.

He adds that the Afghans were 'free from all asperity' towards the non-Muslims as long as they were not at war with that community. The Sikhs and the Afghans had a close history as neighbouring kingdoms since 1748 and most of the time they were adversaries except for the last five years of their close association.

Elphinstone reveals that Shah Zaman, the grandson of Ahmed Shah, allowed the Sikhs 'entire toleration' and 'forbade them to be molested' unless they were enemies. Shah Zaman, we are told was induced by a Mullah to convert two Sikhs and put them to death when the Sikhs refused to convert. The Afghan who told this ordeal to Elphinstone 'expressed a proper sense of cruelty of this proceeding' but applauded the firm resolution of the two Sikhs.

The Afghans hated idol worship but the Hindus were allowed to 'freely exercise their religion' and 'their temples are entirely unmolested'. However, the Hindus were not allowed religious processions and public display of their idols. Although Hindus were considered to be impure by the Afghans and no 'strict man' would consent to eat their meat, they were not 'treated with any particular contempt or hardship'. The Hindus were employed in a position of trust and monetary affairs and seemed to be 'as much at ease' as the majority of the Afghans.

As an example of Afghan toleration, Elphinstone mentions a Sikh goldsmith who was a very intelligent man and had travelled throughout Afghanistan, Persia and Central Asia. This Sikh goldsmith always spoke about 'the kindness and hospitability' of the Afghans as opposed to the Persians who were very suspicious and would not allow the Sikh to draw water from the well or walk in the rain lest he splashed water on a Persian making him impure!

The Hindus had to pay a 'light tax' which Muslims were exempted from. This could be *Jizya*. However, the Mullah and the Qazis could be bigoted too. Elphinstone mentions a Hindu who was forcefully circumcised as he did not get along with the Qazi who swore that the Hindu had converted to Islam and now reverted to idolatry. Over a thousand people gathered and the circumcision was performed with much harshness. The Hindu later fled to Lahore (Ranjit Singh's capital) and returned to Hinduism. It seems strange that this 'Hindu' had previously converted to Islam without circumcision.

Elphinstone adds that in the West Afghanistan, Muslims had no such advantage and Mr Durie related that he had seen many disputes between Hindus and Muslims in Kandahar in which the Hindus were as violent as their opponents without giving the least offence to any of the other Muslims.

In the second edition of his book (Appendix B), Elphinstone has given accounts by a Mr Durie, an Anglo-Indian who lived in Afghanistan as a commoner in the guise of a Muslim. His father was English and a native of Bengal. Durie was employed as a compounder at various dispensaries but then went on travelling. He met Elphinstone and provided some accounts of his own.

In Shor Bazaar of Kabul, there were Hindu shopkeepers among other sellers. Durie informs that there was a passage towards the west of the bazaar that led to 'very high Hindu houses' with a lot of woodwork (signifies residence of rich individuals). From Shor Bazaar to Bala Chowk there were a number of cloth merchants, the majority of who were Hindus.

The city of Kabul had a number of gardens and the road leading to the mountain was excellent. We are told that the houses were 'neatly and cleanly plastered'. The houses were two or three storeys high but the houses of the Hindus were higher and 'greatly consisting of the woodwork'.

Similar to Kabul, the houses of the Hindus were higher and had much woodwork in Ghazni. They were kind to Durie and gave him three or four pices each. One Hindu gave him a pair of shoes and a cotton jacket.

In Kandahar, there were a number of shops run by the Hindus. One night he happened to be at a Hindu's shop when it began to snow. Durie was asked by the Hindus to stay and they brought fire and bread during the night. He mentions visiting Khwaja Khizr, Abasabad and Baba Wali (tomb) at Kandahar.

Durie writes that people passed their time happily and cheerfully. He saw several quarrels among the Muslims and also between Hindus and Muslims which were mostly verbal, sometimes with some blows and wrestling but rarely with bloodshed. In the same breath, we are told that three to four Afghan robbers had their bellies ripped open and were carried on the streets on a camel! A man with a drum told people the reason for their punishment.

Durie stated that both Hindus and Muslims could travel safely but if they had any valuables, they were bound to be robbed of it. The route between Kabul and Kandahar was not defended and robberies were committed frequently. During the Mughal reign, travelling was much safer.

Durie mentions a Khan who 'daily and nightly' melodiously played the Rabab in the company of a baker who sang with great delight. Similarly, some fakirs sang as well. The Hindus sang a variety of music at night and when they visited places of entertainment, they sang and danced.

Durie noticed that a number of Muslims in Peshawar spoke in the Hindustani language although they understood Pashto. They also dressed differently from the Afghans.

Durie probably had certain advantages being an Anglo-Indian with a less pale complexion and knowledge of Indian languages which would have helped him communicating with the Hindu traders.

Account of a Hindu spy

Mohan Lal (1812–77) popularly known as Mohan Lal Kashmiri was a traveller and writer. He travelled to Afghanistan and Central Asia in 1832–34 with Alexander Burnes on a mission given by the East India Company to gain intelligence about the country. His proficiency in the Persian language assisted in this venture. Prof. H.R.

Gupta writes that Mohan Lal faced a lot of problems from fellow Brahmins who disassociated with him as he had lived in Muslim countries for a long period of time. Mohan Lal was perhaps one of the earliest Indian authors to write his memoirs in the English language. He was sent again to Afghanistan during the first Anglo-Afghan war (1838–42) and wrote in detail on Amir Dost Mohammed Khan[2]. However, it is his previous travel to the country in 1832–33 which contains a useful account of the Hindus and the Sikhs there. The book in question, *Travels in the Panjab, Afghanistan and Turkistan to Balk, Bokhara, and Herat; and a Visit to Great Britain and Germany* was published in 1846.

According to this account, the Dakka village at the bank of river Kabul was surrounded by mountains and had soil fit for agriculture. The village had a fountain which had plenty of fish. Mohan Lal writes that for the past two months, two to three people were dying every day due to fever. The people were Afghans (Pashtuns) and spoke Pashto but treated the Hindus badly who had seven houses in the village.

He also visited a Hindu temple with a magnificent building dedicated to Gorakh Nath which was full of pigeons in Jalalabad. The houses in the town were constructed with mud and unburnt bricks but were durable.

Mohan Lal writes that there were 2,000 Hindus in Kabul and 'many of them are the first inhabitants of Kabul'. The Hindus had large families and were 'allowed all the privileges of their religion'. However, the Hindus were distinguished by their robes and painted foreheads.

The Hindu shops were spread over all the streets and bazaars. Although, the local Muslims were prejudiced against them but they treated Hindus 'very tolerantly'.

The great Bamiyan Buddha rock cut statues did not go unnoticed by Mohan Lal. Interestingly, he mentions that the Pandava brothers, immortalised in the Hindu epic *Mahabharata,* visited Bamiyan.

Mohan Lal writes that near the great statue was the mark of a horse's hooves. The Hindus stated that it was the print of Arjun's (one of the Pandavas) horse while the Muslims considered it to be that of Ali's (first Imam). He writes that no history would favour the Hindu account (due to lack of writing) but that the 'tradition speaks in favour of both accounts'.

Haibak (Samangan Province) belonged to Mir Mohammad Murad Beg and the river watered the numerous gardens which 'gives the country a very striking picture'. The caravans of Bukhara and Kabul passed through this region and were required to pay heavy duties. The market was held on Mondays. The Hindus were mostly shopkeepers, spoke Persian and looked very much like the Muslims.

Mohan Lal visited the bazaar on the market-day in Khulm city. There were no proper shops but irregular places which were roofed with mats and wood, not capable of withstanding the rain. Majority of the shops were cloth traders. They were generally Muslims with some Hindus as well.

Mohan Lal mentions a slave boy 'who had a beautiful face' bought by a Hindu banker. The banker loved him like his own son and the boy was well clothed. The boy's pocket was filled with coins to buy whatever he liked and the banker 'diverted him with playful acts'.

The bazaar of Balkh had been described as 'though broad, is irregularly roofed with rafters, bay, and mud'. The bazaar opened on Tuesdays only and rest of the days the shops remained closed! All the shopkeepers were Muslims and the Hindus lived in serais (inns).

The Muslims in the city of Bokhara were not allowed to smoke but the Hindus could smoke in the caravanserai. There were about 3,000 Jews in the city and Mohan Lal appreciated their features and wrote that they looked 'half Scottish'. There were a number of restrictions on the Hindus and Jews who were not allowed to mount on horseback, tie a turban, cloth or shawl around their waist. The Hindus and Jews wore a cloak and skin cap to distinguish them from the Muslims. In contrast the market in Herat was open on Friday and all bargains were managed by twenty Hindu merchants only.

Mohan Lal and Alexander Burnes were on a British mission. While in Mashhad (Persia) they received a letter from John Campell, the British Ambassador to the court of Persia in Tehran that Hindu merchants in Mashhad and Kabul have been asked to supply them with money.

Mohan Lal refers to an interesting story of a bridge called Tirpul built by a benevolent Hindu by the name of Tirat during the reign of Shah Abbas of Iran (1581–1629). Tirat had also built a serai which was occupied by some soldiers when visited by Mohan Lal. The Shah who constructed many inns throughout the country was made aware of Tirat and his charity, so he sent a message to Tirat to receive the money he had spent on the bridge. Tirat refused and said, 'My money is the product of labour and yours of tyranny'.

The ruler was furious upon which Tirat requested that he would submit to the command of the Shah but he would like to visit the bridge with the Shah. Tirat and Shah Abbas came to the bridge and stayed there for a long time. Then Tirat told the Shah that 'he was a dealer in those things which would give eternal happiness in the time to come, and then threw himself into the river'. Everyone, including the Muslims, remembers the benevolence of Tirat and blesses him. Mohan Lal writes that this place was twenty miles from Kosan (Kashan).

On the way to Kabul from Kandahar Mohan Lal came to a small hamlet, named Khail-i-Akhund. He saw a Hindu making his bread, and greeted him saying, *Ram Ram* (Hindu salutation). The Hindu was very surprised to hear this as Mohan Lal was wearing an Afghan Muslim dress.

Mohan Lal then came to a large village called Qilah Jumah (25 miles from Kandahar). Here, he met a Sikh[3] who could not make out if Mohan Lal was a Hindu or Muslim (as he was dressed as such). But following the conversation on religious topics the Sikh was convinced that Mohan Lal was a Hindu.

Account of Alexander 'Bukhara' Burnes

Alexander Burnes was a traveller who made his name by exploring Bukhara, he was even nicknamed Bukhara Burnes[4]. He met and became familiar with a number of Hindu Shikarpuri merchants (from Shikarpur, North Sindh) in Kabul. Burnes writes that the whole trade of Central Asia was in their hands and they had 'houses of agency' from Astrakhan (Southern Russia) and Mashhad (Iran) to Calcutta in Eastern India. Burnes states that they were a plodding (hard working but not imaginative) race and lent money to the Government which gave them protection. They were very tolerable but dressed shabbily. These merchants did not bring their families with them and in Kabul, they had eight great 'houses of agency'. Burnes clarifies that they were 'quite separate from the other Hindu inhabitants' who had 300 families.

Burnes met one of these merchants on the island of Kish in the Persian Gulf. He writes that he was satisfied that they would spread all over Persia and even Turkey. The Jews and Hindus were marked. The former wore a different dress and a conical cap. There were about 4,000 Jews in Bukhara, emigrants from Mashhad (Persia) who were chiefly employed in dyeing cloth. Jews received the same treatment as the Hindus.

There were about 800 Hindus in Bukhara, living in a caravanserai of their own. Burnes writes that they were chiefly natives of Shikarpur and their number had increased in the past few years. The Uzbek and other Muslim merchants found themselves replaced by these people by sheer hard work and as they would 'stake the largest sums of money for the smallest gain'. The Khan of Bukhara, the ruler, lived on the capitation tax which was levied from the Jews and Hindus.

While in Bukhara, Burnes met an army deserter from the East India Company at Bombay (now Mumbai). He was on a pilgrimage to all temples of the Hindu world and was going to the fire temples on the shores of the Caspian Sea!

Burnes quotes Atma Ram, Hindu Prime Minister of the ruler of Bukhara that about 600 families were involved in gold washing business which considerably increased the value of the gold. The Hindu goldsmith bought this gold from villages in Badakhshan and Kafir country (Kafiristan, now called Nuristan) for a small quantity of pepper, coarse cloth, turmeric, glass beads and needles. The market price of gold was much lower in this region compared to Hindustan. These goldsmiths then made a large fortune by selling it in Amritsar (East Punjab).

Burnes in his letter dated 6th December 1837 from Kabul to the Secretary, Government of India, W.H. MacNaghten Esq.[4] writes that Persians had been encouraging the ruler of Bukhara to raise taxes, regiments and force the Hindus to bury their dead or exile themselves. Burnes laments that this would prove 'fatal to the prosperity of Bukhara'. Burnes writes that this policy had been disapproved by Dost Mohammed Khan, Afghan ruler 'as being a variance with the customs of Islam'.

Unlike other accounts, Mohan Lal has mentioned Hindus whom he met in Afghanistan, Iran and Uzbekistan in greater detail. He even met a Sikh near Kandahar. Disappointingly he mentions only one Hindu temple in his memoirs. He was dressed as a Muslim trader which perhaps discouraged him to go near the temples lest it would blow up the disguise.

Alexander Burnes writes that there were 300 Hindu families in Kabul which were in addition to the Shikarpuri merchants who lent money to the Government. These merchants lived separately as they did not bring their families (womenfolk and children) with them to Afghanistan. Burnes' account tells us about the powerful Hindu Prime Minister of the Khan of Bukhara but the city only had Hindu merchants unlike Kabul which had a permanantly settled Hindu population.

References

1. Mountstuart Elphinstone. (1815). *An Account of the Kingdom of Caubul and its Dependencies*. London.
2. Hari Ram Gupta. (1943). *Life and Work of Mohan Lal Kashmiri*. Lahore: Minerva Book Shop.
3. Mohan Lal. (1834). *Journal of a Tour through the Punjab, Afghanistan, Turkistan, to Balk, Bokhara, and Herat; and a Visit to Great Britain and Germany*. Calcutta: Baptist Mission Press; London: Smith, Elder & Co. (1835).
4. Alexander Burnes. (1834). *Travels into Bokhara Vol 1*. London: John Murray.

5. Correspondence relating to Cabul and Afghanistan 1859, copies of the correspondence of Sir Alexander Barnes with the Governor General of India, during his Mission to Cabul, in the years 1837 and 1838, or such part thereof has not already been published.

9

Afghan Hindus and Sikhs in Mid-19th Century

Arthur Conolly's Account

Arthur Conolly was a British explorer and intelligence officer who visited Afghanistan in 1830[1]. He published his memoirs in 1834 and is credited to be the first one to use the term 'The Great Game' to describe the struggle between the British Empire and the Russian Empire for domination over Central Asia. He was put to death by the Amir of Bukhara in 1842 on charges of spying for the British Empire.

While in Tehran, the capital of Persia, Conolly needed 'bills to travel' and Sir John Macdonald referred him to a Hindu banker in the city. However, this banker was in the city of Yezd and while searching for some other merchant in Tehran instead, the city was hit by a severe earthquake which brought the whole business to a standstill.

Conolly mentions that smoking was banned in Bukhara and the offender would be disgraced and made an example of by taking him around the city on a donkey with a plate around his neck!

Conolly was very curious to know the reason behind this prohibition. An Afghan Maulvi who travelled with him from Herat to Kandahar told him 'the blessed Prophet (on whom be God's peace) said, he who makes himself like to those of another tribe becomes as one of that tribe'. The Maulvi argued that as the Shias, Hindus and Jews all smoked, Afghans by smoking would assimilate with them.

Conolly writes that an outside wall built of solid mounds went around Herat. There were thousands of Hindus and almost forty Jewish families settled in Herat. The Hindu merchants refused to assist Conolly! We are told that these Hindu merchants had private houses and some lived in a caravanserai which they owned. A few Hindus ran shops and others 'engaged in the agency and general traffic'. The Hindus were reputed to be rich.

Conolly wonders what encouraged these Hindu merchants to leave their own country and people to come here where they were despised and not allowed many of their religious observations. The climate was also very different and so were the dresses. He answers his own query and states that the lure of big profit brought these people to this country.

Several people in Herat told Conolly an incident about the crown prince of Afghan royalty. A merchant of Bakhtiari tribe gave a Hindu banker 1,800 gold coins for a bill to be exchanged in Kabul. Kamran, the prince, somehow came to know about it and sent a couple of men after him. They started a quarrel with the Bakhtiari merchant and in the ensuing scuffle (purposely) tore away the charm in his neck. The charm had the bill in it. These men then went to the Hindu banker, gave him the bill and forced him to refund the cash and then gave it to their master (the prince).

The Bakhtiari merchant pleaded to the Shah, the ruler, who took pity on him and ordered that he would be paid a rial (still used in Iran) every day from the royal treasury. This was stopped after one week and the merchant was instead ordered to receive a daily portion of bread from the royal kitchen. Even this was stopped after some time and the poor guy remained a beggar outside the palace gates in the hope of getting his money back. He did not get anything and later returned to his own province.

Once Conolly and his Muslim companion were detained at Girishk (120 km northwest of Kandahar) for two nights by two custom officers, a Muslim and a Hindu who 'held the same opinion on the point of honesty'. Conolly did not want their arrival to be noted and passed on to Kandahar after bribing the officers. His companion gave little money and 'many promises of blessings' to his co-religionist but had to give hard cash to the Hindu, 'the only thing that would move him'! They quietly left at eight in the night so that no one saw them departing. The Hindu officer stood on the bridge to see them fairly off.

Conolly writes that all non-Muslims in Kandahar had to pay poll-tax (*Jizya*) in accordance to *Sharia* (Islamic Law) but in the 'disturbed state of the country' every Muslim demanded it of the *kafirs* who paid but got no receipt in return. The *kafir* had to pay as long as he had money and when he had none he had to accept abuses and blows from the 'true believer'.

Conolly states that the Jews were slightly better placed as they had some commonality with the Muslims. They dressed poor and bore injury better than 'any other people in the world'. Neither could the Hindus disguise themselves nor did they try it. They paid the leader of the *Kafilah* (Caravan) which protected them on the road. Sometimes the Hindu had to bribe the police officers and if he couldn't then he was taken to a man of some authority who would torture them until he paid. Conolly sarcastically writes on behalf of these Afghans, 'What treatment could be too bad for such a usurious and in every way abominable, idolater!'

G.T. Vigne's account

In 1836 Godfrey Thomas Vigne visited Afghanistan and wrote a book about it in 1840[2]. He mentions that the Uzbeks in Kunduz city referred to the Hindus as elder brothers and treated them with greater kindness than the other Muslims. The word used was *Lala*. Some Afghans still address Hindus and Sikhs as *Lala,* which means elder brother. However, we must mention here that in December 2016, a prominent Sikh of Kunduz, Lala Dilsoz was killed by assailants.

Vigne is in agreement with Burnes about the population of Kabul being about 60,000 and that the Hindus were few in number and were mainly money-lenders. There were about two hundred houses of Hindus in Bukhara. The ruler had ordered the Hindus to bury, and not cremate their dead and consequently they were leaving the city.

Vigne writes that Uzbeks of Kunduz called Hindus their elder brothers, and treated them with greater kindness than the other Muslims.

Charles Masson's account

James Lewis, a soldier of the British East India Company who became a deserter in 1827, went exploring under the alias Charles Masson and stayed in Afghanistan from 1833–38. He excavated many Buddhist sites in the country and when he returned to England in 1842 he had collected close to 47,000 coins! His memoir was published in four volumes and contains many interesting details on Hindus. It also makes reference to Guru Nanak's place near Jalalabad among other things[3].

Masson mentions that Sultanpur (Nangarhar Province) was famous for orchards and springs and the 'reputed shrine of Baba Nanak'. It is interesting to note that the small town of Sultanpur near Jalalabad was known for its association with Guru Nanak even in the mid-nineteenth century.

Masson reached the small enclosed town of Balla Bagh opposite Adinapur (ancient Jalalabad) which had small remnants of the old city. The place was more commercial than Jalalabad and had many Hindu traders and 'hankers residents' in the town.

Masson writes that Dost Mohammed Khan's (Amir of Afghanistan) authority and stability had assisted the prosperity of Kabul. He was loved by all of his subjects and the Hindus 'fearlessly approach him in his rides, and address him with the certainty of being attended to'.

The Amir administered justice with impartiality and was very attentive to his military. The ruler was conscious about the efficiency of his troops and was very particular about their composition. Due to limited funds and resources, he was not regular in his payments, yet his soldiers seemed satisfied as they knew that 'he neither hoards nor wastes their pay in idle expenses'.

Masson writes that the city of Kandahar was 'regularly built'. The bazaar was 'formed by two lines, drawn from opposite directions, and intersecting in the centre of the place'. Hence the main market was composed of four distinct quarters under different chiefs (Sirdar).

Masson shares his first-hand experience of viewing how the Hindu traders were treated by the three brother chiefs and money was extracted from them. He writes that during his stay 'within the citadel' near Kohan Dil Khan's residence he would see daily visitors as they went to the court of the 'three confederate brothers'. Among the visitors were fifty to hundred Hindu merchants and traders who were forced to come, sometimes dragged along the streets and were asked to furnish money by the chiefs. This was a daily occurrence. Masson wonders how these decent looking men 'submit so patiently to the indignities heaped upon them' and felt that the profit earned in the city must have been enormous for these Hindu merchants lest they would have left the city long ago.

Masson reached the town of Zard (Gami Zard, Helmand province) and went to the house of the Hindu 'who had so civilly entertained us on our first visit' but he was not at home. When he proceeded further to his base camp, he found a couple of Hindus residing there but they did not have any supplies to give or sell.

Masson mentions that towards the eastern part of Kabul was Tappa Mirinjin, the burial place of the Jews and the spot for cremation of the Hindus. The Armenians (who were Christians) had 'their peculiar and walled-in cemetery' near the Muslim graveyards of Khwaja Khedari, south of the Bala Hissar fort. This was directly opposite the 'shrine of Shir Ali Lapchak'. The entrance of the shrine had a marble slab inscription recording the visit of the Mughal Emperor Jahangir to Kabul, on a short pleasure trip in 1002 AH.

Masson later travelled to Jellez, about twenty-seven and a half miles from Kabul. The small town had about eighty houses and two to three Hindu shopkeepers. He adds that in the month of August, Atma Ram, the Hindu *Diwan* of Mir Mahommed Morad Beg, the Uzbek chief of Kunduz, reached Kabul on a mission. He brought twenty-seven horses and twelve sheep, besides clothes and other stuff as presents.

Shakardara is a district in Kabul province. Masson and his party arrived at the large village serai here, inhabited principally by the Hindus, adjacent to which was Sirkh Bolendi (the red mound). A village of a neighbouring district had 150 houses, 'the better of which belong to Hindus, who reside here in some number'.

Bagram is a district in Parwan province. In the small village of Qilla Bolend, resided a few Hindu traders, 'who have considerable intercourse with the neighbouring hill tribes'. They came to a site which the Hindus called Balram and supposed it to have been the capital of Raja Bal.

Masson mentions that in Ghorband (Parwan district, 50 km from Kabul) there was a celebrated Hindu *ziarat* (final resting place of a religious man) which was called Gharuk (Gorakh) Tabbi. Further, they went to a spot called Goraichi which was a place of Hindu pilgrimage. Masson writes, 'we found scratched on the rocks a variety of rude figures of men on elephants and horses, and of men on foot, armed with bows and arrows, of stags and lions, of hares, and other animals'.

Masson mentions how the Amir, Dost Mohammed, reacted when Maharaja Ranjit Singh annexed Peshawar in 1834 while the former was in Kandahar. The Amir declared *Jihad* on the Sikhs and forced the Hindu merchants to pay. Masson mentions how the Mullah of the Amir found approval from the holy book for this act.

He writes, 'With respect to the Hindus, the Khan Mulla's sagacity discovered a sacred text admirably adapted to their case, as well as to the circumstances of the Amir. It set forth, that it was lawful to seize the wealth of infidels, provided the wealth so seized was employed in repelling the aggressions of infidels'.

Both Ranjit Singh and the Amir's Hindu subjects were infidels in the eyes of the Afghans. Masson adds, 'it became obviously consistent with the divine sanction that the Amir should supply his necessities from the funds of his Hindu subjects. Had the Amir possessed a single doubt of conscience it must have been allayed by the sound deductions of the Khan Mulla. The Hindu Shikarpuris, or bankers of the city, were sent for, and being informed they were prisoners until they had arranged to contribute three lakhs of rupees, were made over to the custody of Haji Khan'.

Masson clarifies that this 'financial operation' of the Amir was not restricted to the Hindus but also to rich Muslim merchants and those who were 'politically suspected' or were 'obnoxious' were asked to pay. However, the bulk was paid by the Hindus; the Amir levied two years *Jizya* on them and 'anticipated the receipt of a year's revenue on the town duties of Kabul'.

The city of Peshawar had been a tributary of Maharaja Ranjit Singh since 1818. The Pashtun governors were not removed and they paid tributes to Lahore mostly after some coercion (battles). However, after the annexation of the city by the Maharaja in 1834, Dost Mohammed reacted by declaring *Jihad* (holy war) against Sikhs and found religious sanction to force money from Hindus as both these groups were infidels in their eyes. This perception that infidels are lesser beings which subsided during Amanullah and Zahir Shah resurfaced again in the 1990s and still continues today in Afghanistan.

References

1. Arthur Conolly. (1834). *Journey to the North of India Overland from England Through Russia, Persia, and Affghaunistaun*. London: Richard Bentley.
2. G.T. Vigne. (1840). *Personal Narrative of a Visit to Ghuzni, Kabul and Afghanistan*. London: Whittaker & Co.
3. Charles Masson. (1844). *Narrative of Various Journeys in Balochistan, Afghanistan, the Panjab and Kalat*. London: Richard Bentley.

10

Afghan Sikhs and Hindus in Late 19th and Early 20th Century

The *Sikh Encyclopaedia* mentions that Jaswant Singh (1777–1861), a policeman-turned-saint from East Punjab accompanied by Tahal Singh went to the northwest to preach the Sikh tenants, initially to Peshawar and then to Afghanistan. He stayed in Jalalabad and Kabul for a few years. In Kabul, Gulab Singh became his disciple who was employed in the Afghan cavalry. In the city of Kabul, he came to be known as Khuda Singh. He left Afghanistan in 1834 and settled in Multan[1].

Akali Kaur Singh (1886–1953) also went to Afghanistan for preaching. Khurana writes that he came to Afghanistan for the first time in 1918 and stayed on for a year. He went from house to house preaching the Sikh doctrine which led to the construction of many Gurdwaras especially in places where the Sikhs were in few numbers and were without a place of worship.

Khurana[4] mentions an interesting incident which gives us a glimpse of Akali's personality. Some Mullahs were unhappy with the preaching (though only done among the Sikhs) and they gathered a hostile crowd to chastise the Sikh pontiff but he spoke of brotherhood with them with such humbleness and restraint that the crowd went back satisfied.

Initiation into Khalsa order

Saathi[5] mentions that the first *Amrit Sanchar* (Sikh ceremony of initiation into Khalsa) in Afghanistan was arranged in February 1920 in Lal Pur district in Nangarhar province. A number of *Sahajdhari* took *Khande di Pahul* and became Khalsa. The following year another *Amrit Sanchar* was conducted in the Gurdwara at Lal Pur. It was decided that a Sikh conference would be arranged and all Khalsa and Guru Nanak *Naam Leva* Sikhs (another name for *Sahajdhari* Sikhs) would be invited. During this conference on 22nd January 1921, the *Khalsa Diwan Afghanistan* was created. The organisation played a key part in the social, cultural, economic and political circles of Eastern Afghanistan. They did much work for propagation of the Sikh values and traditions. Saathi credits Akali Kaur Singh's leadership for this achievement. Another Sikh, Teja Singh Swatantar (1901–73) came to Kabul as a Sikh missionary in 1923[6].

Bhai Kahn Singh Nabha was the famous author of *Mahan Kosh,* the first encyclopaedia on Sikhism. It took him thirteen years from 1913–26 to complete it and another four years to publish it. The Maharaja of Patiala got the magnum opus published in 1930. Kahn Singh visited Kabul to attend the Sikh Education Conference (*Samagham*) and reached Kabul on 22nd April 1933. He stayed in the country as a state guest. The Foreign Minister held a banquet in his honour and many local

Afghan Sikhs joined it. Later, Kahn Singh was taken to Dilkhusha Palace to meet Amir Nadir Shah who gifted him among other items, a golden sword. Before leaving Afghanistan, Kahn Singh visited the university, colleges and libraries in the capital. He also visited the Gurdwaras in Kabul, Jalalabad and Sultanpur.

Khurana writes that during the early years of the 20th century, the British established a centre for higher education in Dehradun (Uttarakhand, India), especially for the Afghan elite. Among those who studied here were the future Amir, Nadir Shah and his cousin Shah Wali Khan. During their stay in India, they met Gurbaksh Singh Bedi and became friends with him. In 1929 when Habibullah Kalakani usurped the throne of Kabul, Nadir Shah and his family came to Rawalpindi (West Punjab) where Gurbaksh Singh helped them. He was also a signatory from the British side in the proclamation of freedom of Afghanistan. When Mohd Nadir Shah became the ruler (1929–33) he invited Gurbaksh Singh to the royal palace to stay as a guest. Many local Afghan Sikhs joined him. A Gurdwara was also built in the name of his father, Baba Khem Singh Bedi in Kabul which still exists. In 1962 when Mohd Zahir Shah (son of Mohd Nadir Shah) came to India, he went to meet Brigadier Arvinder Singh Bedi at the National Defence Academy in Pune whom the Shah described as his friend.

The Afghan Sikhs including those in India had very good relations with the royal family in Afghanistan. The above examples where eminent Sikhs were state guests in Afghanistan during the British rule gives an indication of the prestige, influence and respect of the Sikhs in the country.

Sikh Dharamsaals in Uzbekistan & Afghanistan—Late 19th century

Pandit Arjun Muni in his book *Gurdwara Darpan* published in 1929 refers to a number of *Dharamsaals*, their priests and shops around it in Central Asia. He connects these places with the visit of Guru Nanak[7].

Kirpal Singh in *Atlas Travels of Guru Nanak* states that these *Dharamsaals* were built by the Multani and Sindhi Hindu traders who were followers and great admirers of Guru Nanak[8]. This tradition continues till date. *Dharamsaal* is the old name of Gurdwara. The *Sikh Encyclopaedia* notes that Guru Hargobind, the sixth Guru of the Sikhs was the first to use the word Gurdwara for a Sikh place of worship. The information provided by Arjun Muni on the presence of Hindu traders is consistent with the writing of European authors. However, unlike them, reference is made to the *Dharamsaal* or place of worship that invariably would have been built where the majority of devotees resided and ran shops. Giani Gian Singh (1822–1921) makes references to some of these places in his *Tawarikh Guru Khalsa* published in 1891. The account by Arjun Muni has been translated below:

Uzbekistan

Andijan, the city on the eastern edge of the country bordering Kyrgyzstan had a *Dharamsaal* which had a garden with it. There were thirty-five shops of Hindus here. Karmina city also had a *Dharamsaal*. There were seventeen shops of Hindus here who also lit the lamp there. Samarkand had only six shops of Hindus and a *Dharamsaal*. Bukhara however, had the most magnificent *Dharamsaal* and there were almost one hundred Hindu shops.

Afghanistan

Maymana in Faryab province in north Afghanistan had a *Dharamsaal* with an *Udasi* (ascetic order started by Baba Sri Chand) priest. Sherkhan Bandar referred as Karki Bandar by Arjun Muni was the border town of Afghanistan in Kunduz province. There was a *Dharamsaal* here but it had no (permanent) priest. Aqcha in Jowzjan province had a *Dharamsaal* with eleven *bighas* of garden area which was gifted by the local chief (Khan Sahib). There were eleven shops of Hindus here. Whenever a Sadhu or ascetic would visit the *Dharamsaal,* these Hindus would make a collection among themselves and pay for his journey.

Mazar-i-Sharif is the capital of Balkh province and the fourth largest city of Afghanistan. Arjun Muni writes that there was a spring connected with Guru Nanak and Hindus would bathe in it. Tashqurghan now known as Kholm in Balkh province was an ancient town. The town had a *Dharamsaal* with an Arora (Sikh trader caste) Sikh priest. Haibak in Samangan province also had a *Dharamsaal* and so did Kaza (Kaga) in Nangarhar province with a Bedi (same caste as Guru Nanak) priest.

It is equally important that we document the other places in Afghanistan where the Sikhs and the Hindus used to live in the not so distant past. The following information is taken from Khajinder Singh Khurana's book.

The province of Khost is located on the eastern part of Afghanistan which borders FATA in Pakistan. According to Khurana, the province is Pathan dominated and had about 250 Sikh-Hindu houses. The majority of them were Guru Nanak *Naam Leva* or *Sahajdhari* Sikhs. Since time immemorial these people had been eating, dressing and speaking the language of the local Pashtuns. Only a few of them spoke Punjabi. There is one Singh Sabha Gurdwara and a Devi (Goddess) temple in the same complex but in different buildings. Following the partition of the Indian subcontinent into India and Pakistan, some Sikhs and Hindus from the Frontier province in Pakistan crossed over to Khost province in Afghanistan. Following the demolition of Babri Masjid in India in December 1992, a bomb was thrown on the Gurdwara which demolished a part of it.

Pritpal Singh[9] informs that some Hindus from Bannu (Frontier province) in Pakistan crossed over to Khost province in 1947 to escape violence. These people spoke a dialect of Punjabi known as Banwali. A majority of the Banwali Hindus migrated to India in 1947 and were camped in Faridabad near New Delhi. Later, they were given plots there and continue to live there today. They are akin to the Sindhis and have a great reverence for Guru Nanak but would classify themselves as Hindus in the census. They are mostly cloth merchants.

The Banwali-speaking populace that went to Khost after the partition, came to India after 1992 and now are a part and parcel of the Afghan Sikh community in New Delhi. Although most of them are still *Sahajdhari*, they identify themselves as Sikhs. A majority of the traditional Khost community, the Pashto-speaking Sikhs who had been living in Afghanistan for ages have also left the country. The Khost community has built two Gurdwaras in New Delhi. Due to the ongoing war between the Taliban and the Afghan government forces in Khost province, the remaining Pashto-speaking community resettled in Kabul and number around forty. They are all men except two or three families. These men have sent their families either to India or abroad and are working in their shops, alone in Afghanistan.

Tsamkani (or Chakmani) is a district in Paktia province which is next to Khost. It had an old Gurdwara dedicated to Guru Nanak. The Sikhs from Khost, Gardez and nearby areas would come on *Puranmashi* (full moon), *Sangrand* (first day of the Sikh traditional calendar) and *Gurpurabs* (days associated with the Sikh Gurus like their birthdays, etc.). Khurana writes that in 1947, it was rebuilt. People believed that childless couples, who prayed and did *Ardas* here, were blessed with a child. Baba Krishna, a famous person of Kandahar was blessed with a boy and he made him a *Keshdhari* Sikh.

Every year special week-long religious programmes were arranged during *Vaisakhi* and the Sikhs would come from far-off places. As per tradition when the

Khalsa flag (*Nishaan Sahib*) is changed, the congregation fire in the air to express their delight!

Gardez, the capital of Paktia province, had about a hundred homes of the Sikhs and Hindus. The city has a Singh Sabha Gurdwara and a temple. Even prior to 1991 most of these people shifted to Kabul and in 1992 to India and other foreign countries. The city has a stream and locals believe that Guru Nanak came here during his fourth *Udasi* and associate the stream to him.

In the olden times, there were 100–150 homes of Sikhs and Hindus in the Logar province. It is said that Guru Nanak came in the Babus region and the soft water stream is connected to him. In 1932 due to the fighting between the Mangal and Jajian tribes, most of the Sikhs and Hindus left for Kabul. There is a Gurdwara in the town of Baraki Rajan.

Kalangar has a Hindu pilgrimage place known as Gorakh Tibba on top of a hill. There is a cave temple in the Avjosh Mountain dedicated to Goddess Singhwani.

Lashkargah, the capital city of Helmand province has two Gurdwaras namely Guru Singh Sabha Gurdwara and Nanak Nirankari Gurdwara built around 1975 and 1980 respectively. Unfortunately, only two Sikhs are left in Helmand now. These are the shopkeepers who have sent their families to India and are running their small businesses and looking after the Gurdwaras[10].

The Sikh surnames in Helmand and Kandahar were generally Gandhi (numerous), Chandori, Khattar,

Popli, Kukreja, Aneja, Taneja, Bhatia and Khatri (numerous).

Jalalabad, the capital of Nangarhar province, had a population of 12,000 Sikhs. Until 1931 Sikhs and Hindus were settled throughout the village and towns of Nangarhar and in the neighbouring Kunar province. That year during an attack by the robbers, two robbers and a Sikh were killed. This meant an ongoing enmity between the robbers and the Sikhs. The government relocated the Sikhs and Hindus to the cities. The majority of them came to Jalalabad which significantly increased their population in the city. Two magnificent Gurdwaras and a temple exist in Jalalabad and two in Sultanpur.

As per the list given in the book *Ithas Khalsa Diwan Afghanistan* by Sadhu Singh Saathi, they are: Gurdwara Guru Nanak Darbar, Gurdwara Guru Tegh Bahadur, Guru Asthan, Sultanpur and Guru Asthan Sri Chashma Sahib, Sultanpur. In addition, there are fifteen Singh Sabha Gurdwaras in Nangarhar and Kunar provinces. Laghman province has six Singh Sabha Gurdwaras.

Ghadar Party and Afghanistan

The Ghadar Party was formed by Sikhs settled in North America during the First World War (1914–18) to start a mutiny in British Indian army and end the colonial rule in India. These rebels (freedom fighters) were largely from the Punjabi Sikh community but leaders came from diverse backgrounds including Hindus and Muslims from other states of India. Their members tried to spark a rebellion in the British garrisons in India, Burma and Singapore among other countries. After the war, a major conspiracy was discovered involving Germany and the Ghadar Party. The rebellion failed and many were given death penalties, life sentences and confiscation of the property for 'waging a war against the Emperor'.

Afghanistan also featured prominently in this rebellion. In December 1915, a government-in-exile of Free Hindustan was established in Kabul. This government-in-exile tried to establish contacts with anti-British countries like Turkey, Germany, Japan and China among others. Initially, the Afghan government supported the mission as they had a common cause (independence from the British) but later under pressure from the British, the offices of the government-in-exile were closed[10]. However, the Ghadar Party members remained active in Afghanistan.

Although Afghanistan was not a colony like India, the country was a British protectorate state and the British indirectly ruled it. The British had full control over its foreign affairs and a group of advisers oversaw the Afghan government. Afghanistan had some internal autonomy similar to the princely states in India. The Afghans celebrate 19th August as their independence day to commemorate the Treaty of Rawalpindi signed between the Afghans and the British in August 1919, following the third Anglo-Afghan war. A complete sovereignty was achieved in October 1921 when the British and the Afghans signed the Treaty of Independence in India and within a few months Afghanistan established diplomatic relations with Soviet Russia.

The Afghan Sikhs became members of the Afghanistan Ghadar Party and actively participated in the freedom struggle. The India Intelligence Bureau issued a *Ghadr Directory* in 1917 and then updated it in 1934 which contains the names of persons who have taken part in the Ghadar movement in America, Europe, Africa, Afghanistan and India. The directory contains names of many Afghan Sikhs, for example Bahadur Singh, Chanda Singh, Dhian Singh, Narain Singh, Sarup Singh and Sundar Singh (all from Lal Pur district in Nangarhar province). There were Afghan Sikhs from Kabul and even Ghazni in that list.

One interesting entry was that of Bawai Singh alias Gurmukh of Charbagh (Laghman province) who was a *Granthi* (priest) at the local Gurdwara. We are told he was a 'firebrand' member of the Afghanistan Ghadar Party and visited India in April 1931. He was a good speaker and addressed public meetings in his Gurdwara and other places[12].

References

1. Giani Pratap Singh. (1962). *Jivan Baba Khuda Singh Ji Lahore Vale*. Amritsar.
2. Khajinder S. Khurana. (2001). *Kabul de Sangat tee Afghanistan da Sankhep Ithas* (in Punjabi). Delhi.
3. Sadhu Singh Saathi. (1994). *Ithas Khalsa Diwan Afghanistan*. Jalalabad: Parchar Committee Khalsa Diwan Afghanistan.
4. Harbans Singh. (1992–98). *Encyclopaedia of Sikhism*. Patiala: Punjabi University.

5. Ganda Singh (Ed.). (1969). *'Iraq, Iran aate Afghanistan vich Guru Nanak de Sthaan'. Sources on the Life and Teaching of Guru Nanak: The Punjab Past and Present, Vol. 3.* Patiala: Punjabi University.
6. Fauja Singh and Kirpal Singh. (1969). *Atlas Travels of Guru Nanak.* Patiala: Punjabi University.
7. London-based Afghan Sikh, Pritpal Singh who made the famous documentary *Mission Afghanistan.*
8. Information provided by the New Delhi-based Shamsher Singh who left Helmand in the late 2016.
9. K.H. Ansari. (1986). *Pan-Islam and the Making of the Early Indian Muslim Socialist. Modern Asian Studies.* Vol. 20, no. 3, pp. 509–537. London: Cambridge University Press.
10. The Director, Intelligence Bureau, Home Department. (1934). *The Ghadr Directory.* Patiala: Government of India Press, Reprint Punjabi University (1997).

11

Gurdwaras in Afghanistan

The places of worship of minorities hold a very important place for them as they also serve the role of community centres. Afghanistan has always been a conservative society and like the majority Muslim community, the Afghan Sikhs and Hindus were also very close to their faith. Even now in India, Germany, UK and the rest of Europe, the Afghan Sikhs continue to be *Keshdhari*[1].

Prof. Ganda Singh visited Afghanistan in 1952 to research on Ahmed Shah Abdali. He visited Kandahar, Kabul, Ghazni and Jalalabad among other places and visited the Gurdwaras in each city. His memoir, *Afghanistan da Safar* written in Punjabi is of huge value to understand the status of Afghan Sikhs and Hindus in the country during that time[2]. The memoir provides the history of each Gurdwara he visited. Certain sections are briefly translated below:

In Kandahar, there were about 2,500 (1952) Sikhs and *Sevaks*. The *Keshdhari* were known as Sikhs and *Sahajdhari*[3] (shaven) were known as *Sevaks*. There was little socio-cultural difference between the two groups.

Most of these people (Sikh, *Sevak* and Hindu) were traders and shopkeepers. Some of them were *Hakeems*

(Greco-Arabic physicians, locals called it Unani-Tibb). However, there were no tailors and carpenters among them. Their ladies kept *purdah* (veil) which is a national custom. The elderly Muslim ladies practised *chadar da purdah* (outer garment or open cloak worn by women where the face is visible) and younger ones wore *burqa* (only eyes are visible). The Sikh and Hindu ladies irrespective of their age practised *chadar da purdah*.

Prof. Ganda Singh was critical of the level of education among the Afghan Sikhs and Hindus in Kandahar. He writes that the boys of the two communities seldom went to government colleges. The community had opened a primary school but it was not in a very good condition. The boys did not go to high schools lest the Government (of Afghanistan) sent them abroad for higher education (which was a norm). Due to this oversight, the Sikh-Hindu community was behind Muslims in education and they were thus, neither seen nor heard in government and administrative circles. The Prof. adds that the Government was not to be blamed for it; the Sikhs and Hindus themselves were responsible for it.

Prof. Singh laments that there was no famous person among the Sikh-*Sevak* community of Kandahar. They were simply traders who were busy with their businesses. He could not find a single person who took an active part in social, cultural or administrative circles. He adds that Kandahar had some Hindu temples. One Devi Mandir (temple dedicated to Goddess) was very famous. There were five Gurdwaras which were known as *Dharamsaal* [4]. He visited them on 5th September 1952.

Dharamsaal Siri Guru Nanak was based in Kabuli Bazaar and was said to be built by Baba Jaspat. He was from the family of Baba Sahib Singh Bedi of Una whose family line went as,

1. Baba Jaspat
2. Baba Sangat Baksh
3. Baba Devi Chand
4. Baba Ishar Das
5. Baba Hari Chand
6. Baba Jagdish (incumbent in 1952).

According to Baba Jagdish, he was a descendant of Guru Nanak from the family at Dera Baba Nanak and his family line was related to Baba Sahib Singh Bedi. According to Khurana, Baba Lakhi was the *parbandak* (administrator/organiser) until 1990[5].

Suthrian di Dharamsaal in Shikarpuri Bazaar was commonly known as the *Dharamsaal* of Baba Hari Shah and he was the main *parbandak*. Baba Kangaal Shah first came here. The family line is as follows:

1. Baba Kangaal Shah
2. Baba Aatam Shah
3. Baba Partap Shah
4. Baba Puran Shah
5. Baba Sampuran Shah
6. Baba Akhat Shah

7. Baba Sant Shah
8. Baba Hari Shah (incumbent in 1952).

Baba Hari Shah told the Professor that Baba Aatam Shah was cremated in India hence there was no *samadhi* (tomb) for him. But *samadhi* of all the other priests were there. Basically, there were *Guthay Nishaan* (symbolic signs such as stone) and nothing else. Baba Hari Shah would do *Katha* (discourse) of Guru Granth Sahib every morning and a considerable *Sangat* (Sikh congregation) would gather at the *Dharamsaal*. There was a handwritten copy of the Guru Granth Sahib at the *Dharamsaal*. According to Khurana, the last *parbandak* was Baba Krishan and the *Sangat* would gather twice a day.

Waadi Dharamsaal, Shikarpuri Bazaar was famous as the *Dharamsaal* of Baba Siri Chand, the son of Guru Nanak and founder of Udasi Sect, who visited Afghanistan. The word *Waadi* means bigger. There was an old handwritten copy of Guru Granth Sahib which was written in Samvat 1725 or 1668 CE during the time of the ninth Guru, Tegh Bahadur.

Post-1992, when the Hindus and Sikhs of Kandahar left and went to India they started to refer to *Dharamsaal* as Gurdwara. Now, this is also known as Gurdwara Baba Sri Chand. This place of worship is now closed but under the possession of a *Sangat*. Shamsher Singh, an Afghan Sikh now residing in New Delhi, from Lashkargah (Helmand province) visited it in 2016 and made a short video of children performing *Keertan* (singing compositions from Guru Granth Sahib).

Shamsher Singh informs that due to lack of *Sangat* the Gurdwara Baba Sri Chand has been closed for over two decades. Only when a *Sangat* visits that they perform the *Keertan*.

The *Chotti Dharamsaal* also at Shikarpuri Bazaar has no information on who built it and when. *Chotti* literally means small. Baba Harnam Das, the incumbent *parbandak* at the time told the Professor whatever he remembered. The succession line of the priests was as follows:

1. Shha
2. Sanpat
3. Tehal Das
4. Khushal Das
5. Bhagat Bawar
6. Harnam Das.

Baba Harnam Das only remembered that this *Dharamsaal* was built before the reign of Amir Abdul Rahman Khan (1880–1901). There were two handwritten copies of Guru Granth Sahib here. According to Khurana, the last *parbandak* was Baba Parmanand until 1990 who then left Afghanistan and came to India.

Enquires sent to Kandahar[6] state revealed that there are ten Afghan Hindus living in one of the Gurdwaras (in absence of homes) and they perform the *Prakash* and *Sukh Aasan* of the Guru Granth Sahib[7]. It is the only functional Gurdwara in Kandahar at the moment.

Dharamsaal of Masands had no one who could provide some background information on it. The Professor writes that the main *parbandak* was Bhai Mohan whose brother's name was Bhai Ram. There was no *Prakash* of the Guru Granth Sahib performed here. The Professor found that in one of the rooms, there were two barbers who had come from India for employment and would leave after staying for some time. The Masands were originally the preachers nominated by the early Sikh Gurus. By the time of Guru Gobind Singh, the Masands had become corrupt and the Guru abolished this institution.

According to Khurana, most of the Sikhs in Kandahar were *Sahajdharis*. However, a few Sikhs lived in the villages near Kandahar who were *Keshdharis*.

Enquires from Kandahar reveal that this *Dharamsaal* has allegedly been sold and the new Afghan Muslim owner has built an additional storey on the existing structure. A Gurdwara is considered as the property of the whole *Sangat* hence this is unusual. Isher Dass in his book mentions that Gurdwaras and Hindu temples in Afghanistan were registered in individual or family names and were subject to taxation[8]. Hence, this allegation may not be improbable. However, a number of Gurdwaras and Mandirs are under illegal occupation of the majority community and when challenged they tend to state that they have purchased it.

Regarding Ghazni, the Professor writes that there were a few Sikh-Hindu shopkeepers and about fifty to sixty houses in the city. Their population was about 300. We are told that Bhai Dayal Singh Tabib and Bhai Teja Singh Tabib were famous personalities from the community. The city had an old Gurdwara that the Professor visited on 7th September 1952. The Gurdwara had seven old handwritten copies of the Guru Granth Sahib and one Dasam Granth. On four of the *birs* (Guru Granth Sahib) was *Samvat* 1811, 1814, 1821 and 1825 *Bikrami* (1754, 1757, 1764 and 1768 CE) written on them. The copy of the Dasam Granth Sahib had *Zafarnama* and *Hikyatan* in Persian script.

The second one, Gurdwara Kotla Sahib was located two kilometres away on a hill outside Ghazni city. The last information received from Afghanistan states that the Gurdwara is now closed due to lack of *Sangat* and opened only when the Sikh devotees come to visit it.

Prof. Ganda Singh writes that the city of Jalalabad had about 260 houses of Sikh and *Sevaks* and a population of 1,500. Most of them were traders. At one time, there was a sizable population of Sikh-*Sevaks* in nearby villages who had not settled in the city. However, in 1952 there were very few Sikhs or Hindus in the villages.

Jalalabad has a big Gurdwara Sahib (Guru Nanak Darbar) under the management of *Khalsa Diwan*. This is the centre of *Khalsa Diwan Afghanistan* which is an organisation of forward thinking Sikhs. The Professor writes that their members are responsible Sikhs who have dedicated their lives to the Sikh community. Bhai Darbari Singh was the President and Babu Saran Singh was the Vice-President and both were very enthusiastic and had taken a lot of initiatives for the welfare of the Sikh community. Saathi writes that in 1936, the *Khalsa Diwan Afghanistan* decided to open schools in all the Gurdwaras to impart religious education to the kids. The *Khalsa Dharmik* school was opened on the first floor of Guru Nanak Darbar. All Gurdwaras under *Khalsa Diwan*

Afghanistan were instructed to open similar schools in their Gurdwaras.

The Professor mentions that the Gurdwara came under the plan for a new road in the city and consequently some parts of it were demolished by the government. The Sikhs became anxious and sought redressal; thereafter the government changed the plan bypassing the Gurdwara. A new beautiful building was built later.

Jalalabad like Kandahar had an Indian consulate which looked after the trade and other interests of the Indians and also provided passport and travel facilities.

About eight miles north-west of Jalalabad, in Sultanpur city, there is a *chashma* (spring) associated with Guru Nanak known as Chashma Sahib. The Professor writes that there is no Gurdwara there, just a government building with walls and no roof. However, there are two concrete *sarovars* (pool of water). There were twenty-three houses of Sikhs and Hindus around and their population was about a hundred.

After Baba Karam Singh Bedi, the main *parbandak* was his nephew Baba Bhagwan Singh followed by Baba Jawahar Singh Bedi. At that time there was no *Prakash* of the Guru Granth Sahib. When in 1906 Amir Habibullah Khan came here, he was very impressed by the scenic beauty of the place and asked the Sikhs to sell it. They expressed their inability as it belonged to all the Sikhs of the world as Guru Nanak had visited it. The Amir got angry when the Sikhs did not relent. He forcibly occupied it and built an impressive building.

The Sikhs stopped coming except during the summer when the Amir would leave for Kabul. The Sikhs would then bribe the soldiers and get *jal* (water) of the *chashma* for drinking but were not allowed to bathe in it. This continued until 1919.

When Amanullah Khan, son of Habibullah Khan became the Amir, a deputation was sent to him by the Sikhs and he listened to them very patiently, finally allowing them to bathe in the *chashma*. In 1924, Master Udham Singh, a Punjabi Sikh along with other important Sikhs of Afghanistan got permission to hold a *Diwan* (religious program, audience hall) on *Vaisakhi* (major Sikh festival in April, commemorates the birth of Khalsa order in 1699). The military commander, Sardar Nadir Khan (later Amir Mohd Nadir Shah) had a big hand in this approval. The Professor wrote that he is remembered with great respect by the Sikhs even now.

The building was subjected to loot and arson in 1928–29 during civil disturbances as it was the Amir's property. Ganda Singh writes that now only the walls remain. *Khalsa Diwan* continued to hold *Vaisakhi Diwan* every year with the help of the local authorities. Even government officials join the celebrations (Saathi writes that this started from 1926). A lot of Sikh marriages are conducted during this programme. These are no cost marriages where the *Guru ka Langar* (community kitchen) is continuously served. The *Khalsa Diwan* (organising body) would take a token amount, equivalent of rupees five for *Karah Parshad*[9]. Saathi in his book records that *en masse* marriages started from 1934. On the main road, *Langar* was served to all people irrespective of their religion. The Professor notes that Bhai Bahadar Singh had slowly sold off his property to finance the *Langar*. The city also has an old historical Gurdwara.

The Professor writes that in Kabul there were about 850 houses of Sikhs and Hindus, known as Sikh and *Sevak* respectively, who have great reverence for the Gurdwara. They number about 4,000. The Professor adds there are a few Hindus here who have been living in Kabul since the olden times even before the advent of Islam and were racially, pure Afghans. The old Kabul city also had some Hindu and Gujjar residents.

Prof. Ganda Singh explains that when Guru Nanak came to Afghanistan the Hindus became his disciples that is Sikh-*Sevaks* and this continues till date. The Sikh history tells us that the Sikh *Sangat* from Kabul, Ghazni and Kandahar came to Punjab many times to visit the Gurdwaras. Their love and respect continued to grow unlike other countries and during Guru Gobind Singh's time, they became Singh (Khalsa). With time, due to the long distance from Punjab, many *Sangats* have no remaining *Amritdhari* (baptised) within them but their love and respect towards the Sikh tenants did not decrease. They are known as *Sevaks*. They do everything according to *Rehat Maryada* (Sikh Code of Conduct) and consider only the Guru Granth Sahib as their God.

The Professor adds that there are some old Hindus who believe in and recite the Guru Granth Sahib but they also go to Hindu temples for *puja* (worship).

There is no discord between the Sikhs and the *Sevak* brotherhood. Wherever there are Sikhs and *Sevaks,* there are Gurdwaras. There are seven in Kabul, five in Kandahar, and one each in Ghazni, Jalalabad and Sultanpur. There are Gurdwaras in small towns and villages as well.

The Professor wrote that the Sikhs in Afghanistan have great respect for the religion and there was hardly anyone who missed the morning congregation at the Gurdwara. *Asa di Waar* and *Katha/Keertan* were performed and *Gurpurabs* were celebrated with great fervour. Most of them were *Amritdhari*. At some places everyone, including children and seniors, were *Amritdhari*. One of the famous Sikhs of Kabul was Baba Saran Singh Bedi. Due to his efforts, a religious and Gurmukhi school for Sikh children was established. There was also a facility for teaching Hindi.

Unfortunately, the oldest historical Gurdwara of Afghanistan, Gurdwara Guru Nanak, based in Jad Mewan was demolished when the road was widened in 1950. As per the regulations, the dismantled material and cost of the land was paid to the Gurdwara Management Committee. They could have re-purchased the land as not all was lost to the road. After some time, it was purchased by a good-natured local Muslim who was willing to sell it to the Kabuli Sikhs. However, the local Sikhs did not get together to raise the amount to buy the land.

The Jalalabad-based Sikh organisation, *Khalsa Diwan Afghanistan,* volunteered to help in it. The Professor writes that he was told by a Kabuli Sikh that they did not require the help of outsiders (i.e. Jalalabad). Sadly, the local Kabuli Sikhs never got together to rebuild this Gurdwara. Sixty-nine years have lapsed and soon the generation which knows the exact location of the Gurdwara commemorating the visit of Guru Nanak in Kabul will be gone.

It is still, not too late. The resilient Afghan Sikh community living abroad has helped their fellow Sikh brothers to repair and rebuild almost all Gurdwaras in Kabul as they had been heavily damaged during the civil war. If the required awareness is raised about this Gurdwara, the community can be counted upon to make a donation.

After the Gurdwara Guru Nanak, Prof. Ganda Singh writes that Gurdwara Khalsa (Dera Bhai Gurdas) in Shor Bazaar is the oldest one. During the time of Guru Hargobind (1606–44), Bhai Gurdas came here and it was built at that time. At that time it was a double-storey building. The upper storey had the Gurdwara and Diwan Hall. The ground floor was known as Bhai Gurdas Dera which also had *Prakash* of the Guru Granth Sahib and an *Akhand Jyot* (eternal flame) there. On the top of *Sunehri lakar* (golden wood), it was written *Dhan* (praiseworthy and blessed) Guru Hargobind Sahib *Ji*. A handwritten copy of Dasam Granth written in Samvat 1769 (1712 CE) resided here. According to Khurana, in 1987 a twenty-one member committee was formed to begin a new building for the Gurdwara Sahib.

As per the British Embassy in Kabul, the Gurdwara served as a Sikh school in the past and now accommodates around ten families on a permanent basis[10]. This is one of the three Gurdwaras in Kabul which are fully functional.

The Gurdwara Baba Siri Chand in Shor Bazaar was established by Baba Almast when he came here, writes the Professor. He was an *Udasi* Sadhu (ascetic) of Baba Siri Chand and chief of the *Udasi Dhuahh* sect. He was born and brought up in Srinagar, Jammu and Kashmir in *Samvat* 1610 *Bikrami* (1553 CE) in the house of Gorr Brahmin Hardit. The famous *Udasi* priest Balu Hasna was his younger brother. He established a number of centres of Sikhi and Gurdwaras in India. The *Dharamsaal* of Baba Siri Chand was also established by him. There were two handwritten copies of the Guru Granth Sahib and one of them is dated *Samvat* 1918 *Jeth* 25 (or 1861 CE).

Dass writes that the new building was completed in late 1991. This Gurdwara was the last place of worship which was rebuilt by the Hindus and Sikhs before the Mujahideen came to power. As per the British Embassy in Kabul, it currently houses five Sikh-Hindu families on a permanent basis.

The Gurdwara Baba Ganj Baksh is named after Baba Ganj Baksh from Gurdaspur, an important *Udasi* Sadhu who became a Sikh during the time of Guru Amardas (1552–74) and started preaching. His followers are known as Ganj Bakshiye. The main *parbandak* was Bhai Lachman Das. He remembers the line of *Mahants* until *Mahant* Badri Nath. When the Professor visited, the incumbent was *Mahant* Trilok Nath. Here is the line of *Mahants*:

1. Mahant Badri Nath
2. Mahant Ram Nath (son)
3. Mahant Prem Nath (son)
4. Mahant Trilok Nath (son).

The Gurdwara had three handwritten copies of the Guru Granth Sahib and one of them was dated 1806 *Katak* (1749 CE). It is alleged that the Sikh(s) owner of the Gurdwara rented the property when they left the country. Information from Kabul states that this small Gurdwara is now under the illegal occupation of the tenant who belongs to the majority community.

The Gurdwara Jyoti Saroop in Lahori Darwaza, the Professor writes, is known as such because of the presence of an *Akhand Jyot* (eternal flame). The main *parbandak* was Bhai Uttam Chand who was forty-four years old then. He remembered the names of the previous two *parbandaks,* Bhai Pokhar Singh and Bhai Lachman Das. There was a small mosque behind the Gurdwara of a Hindu *fakir* Chacha Bali who was revered by both the Muslims and Hindus. When he died, he was buried and later they built a mosque over his grave. In 1919, the wall between the Gurdwara and the mosque fell down and the Muslims did not allow the Sikhs to repair it. Amanullah Khan tried to persuade the Muslims but they did not allow him to intervene and said it was a matter of *Deen* (religion) and only the Emperor could intervene. Later, when Amanullah became the Amir he himself supervised and commissioned the wall. The Gurdwara had a handwritten copy of the Guru Granth Sahib dated *Samvat* 1904 (1847 CE).

This Gurdwara was badly destroyed during the civil war and has been repaired since. It is now empty and a Muslim watchman looks after the property[11].

The Gurdwara Baba Gurbaksh Singh in Kandhari Kuccha, Hindu Gujjar was established when Baba Gurbaksh Singh Bedi visited the place. He like his father Sir Khem Singh Bedi went on Sikh preaching tours to distant places. He also came to Kabul. The Professor notes that next to the Gurdwara was the residence of Baba Saran Singh Bedi, Headmaster of the *Guru Nanak Dharmik* school. A handwritten copy of the Guru Granth Sahib was placed in the Darbar. Currently, this Gurdwara is empty and the local *Sangat* knows it by the name of Gurdwara Baba Khem Singh.

The Gurdwara Bhai Pirana in Saria Lahoriya is named after Bhai Pirana, a famous Sikh and a preacher during the time of Guru Arjan and Guru Hargobind. He was both a saint and a soldier. He fought very bravely alongside Guru Hargobind in the battles against the Mughals. He was also at service of Guru Hargobind when the Guru was imprisoned in Gwalior by the Mughal Emperor Jahangir. It also has a handwritten copy of the Guru Granth Sahib.

According to Khurana, in 1986 this Gurdwara was merged with Guru Har Rai Sahib Gurdwara and a magnificent new building was created. Till 1986, Bhai Ishar Singh Longani took care of this Gurdwara.

The Gurdwara Guru Har Rai Sahib in Shor Bazaar is in the name of the seventh Sikh Guru, Guru Har Rai (1644–61). It was established in memory of his

Sikh Bhai Goinda. This was the *Manji* (preaching centre) place of Bhai Goinda. Two handwritten copies of the Guru Granth Sahib were in the Gurdwara.

Sangat Singh mentions an interesting event which is also quoted by Khurana regarding this Gurdwara. A Hindu priest once placed some idols in the Gurdwara and would not remove them even when requested by the Sikhs. The matter was taken to Amir Abdul Rahman Khan who after careful consideration made a clear distinction between the Hindu and the Sikh religion. In his judgement in 1905, the Amir said the Sikhs were 'the followers of Baba Nanak who was one of the greatest Unitarians and was opposed to idol worship'. The Amir also added that 'Hindus had no concern with Sikh shrines, as Sikhs had nothing to do with Hindu Thakurdwaras or Shivdwaras'[12].

According to Khurana, in 1982 a large portion of the Gurdwara Sahib was lost due to the planning of the new enlarged road. The organisers of the Gurdwara then bought the nearby houses and made a big and magnificent building. They included a lodging place for tourists, dispensary and library. The Stage Secretary of the Gurdwara, Gajinder Singh became a Member of Parliament in 1977 under the Najib government. The original *Manji* (cot) of Bhai Goinda was transferred to India in 1992 and is currently preserved in a Gurdwara built by the Afghan Sikhs at Greater Kailash, New Delhi.

The Gurdwara was occupied by Ahmed Shah Massoud, a warlord from the Northern Alliance and almost destroyed in the civil war and partially rebuilt in 2001. It was completely renovated and new quarters were built in 2014. As per the British Embassy in Kabul, fifteen Sikh-Hindu families are permanently living in it.

The Gurdwara Bhai Mansa Singh was a small Gurdwara built by Bhai Mansa Singh, a devout Sikh in Kabul. Later, Baba Chet Singh, another devout Sikh bought more land and enlarged it. There were four handwritten copies of the Guru Granth Sahib and two copies of the Dasam Granth here. One of the copies of the Guru Granth Sahib was dated *Samvat* 1795 (1738 CE) and mentions the Khalsa.

This Gurdwara was destroyed during the civil war and rebuilt by the Afghan Sikhs who claim ancestry from Multan. The British Embassy in Kabul reported that currently, ten Sikh-Hindu families are living in it.

The Gurdwara Singh Sabha in Karte Parwan is the largest Gurdwara in Kabul. Both Isher Dass and Khurana write that in 1965, several Sikh and Hindu families bade the old city parts of Kabul, such as Shor Bazar and Hindu Gozer farewell and inhabited the new neighbourhoods. They were able to obtain permission from Zahir Shah's government to build a Gurdwara in the district of Karte Parwan. The Gurdwara had three floors and a basement, including a kitchen, a primary school building, an emergency clinic and a guest house. It currently hosts four families.

Narinder Pal Singh from Kabul has informed that *Prakash* (installation) of the Guru Granth Sahib in the morning is performed in three Gurdwaras in Kabul namely Gurdwara Singh Sabha in Karte Parwan, and Gurdwara Khalsa and Gurdwara Guru Har Rai Sahib, both in Shor Bazar.

The Gurdwara Baba Almast is a small Gurdwara near the Khalsa Gurdwara and is connected to it through the back lane. It was originally built and run by the Sikhs who were goldsmiths by profession. Following the civil war, this was rebuilt and now two Sikh families live in it. They perform the *Prakash* daily and bring the Guru Granth Sahib into the Darbar on Sunday for the benefit of the *Sangat*[13].

The Gurdwara Kotha Sahib is located forty-five miles north of Kabul in a town called Aakasrai. It is said that Bhai Sharda Singh was blessed with the *darshan* (auspicious sight) of Guru Gobind Singh. He then converted his house into a Gurdwara and started preaching. The Gurdwara was damaged during the civil war in 1929 and rebuilt by the *Sangat*. Before 1992, the *Sangat* would come in huge numbers on full moon day. An annual three-day programme was arranged which was well attended by the *Sangat*. Before 1992, almost 800 to 900 Afghan Sikhs and Hindus lived in the town. It is now abandoned and the building is in shambles[14]. It has been alleged that the land and the building of Gurdwara Sahib has been illegally occupied by miscreants from the majority community[15].

Sikhs and Hindus in the country

According to Prof. Ganda Singh, there were about 6,000–7,000 Sikhs and Hindus[16] in the country who lived mainly in Kabul, Kandahar, Jalalabad, Ghazni and other cities. A few of them lived in villages as well. They were all Afghans and had religious freedom to eat, drink and perform their rituals.

The Professor writes that there was free education for all until University and Islamic study was compulsory but in the big cities where the Sikhs, Hindus and Jews were in appreciable numbers community teachers were appointed so that they could teach their respective religion to their students.

The Professor adds that the Pashtun nationalism was very high at the time of his visit. He adds that the Afghans were famous for entertaining their guests. He was treated with much compassion and respect. The Professor met with communal behaviour at very few places which he felt was due to the Pakistani propaganda against Indians especially the Sikhs[17].

The dates on the handwritten copies of the Guru Granth Sahib are yet another proof of the antiquity of Sikhs in Afghanistan. The Professor visited the house of one Kartar Singh, who lived in the Hindu Gujjar area of Kabul and possessed a copy of the Guru Granth Sahib which had the signature of Guru Gobind Singh (1675–1708). The Professor gave a logical explanation that some devotees from Afghanistan took *birs* of the Guru Granth Sahib with them when they went to meet the Sikh Gurus in Punjab and for posterity someone may have got the signature. There are numerous instances in Sikh history when *Sangat* from Kabul came to Punjab to meet the Gurus. This has been covered in other chapters.

Zahedan in Iran is a border town to Afghanistan and Pakistan. Prof. Ganda Singh had a connecting flight here. He writes that a few Sikhs and Hindus lived in the city and Harbans Singh was a famous personality among them. They were mostly traders and there was one Gurdwara which had the facility for devotees to stay overnight. This Gurdwara still exists and there is another one in the capital, Tehran[18]. Iranian Professor, Farideh Okati, states that Sikhs came to Zahedan in the early part of the 20th century when the British decided to extend the railway line from India to this broder town and along with the local languages of Persian, Balochi and Sistani, they were proficient in Punjabi. By 1947 there were a hundred Sikh families in the city but half of them went to Tehran after the Iranian revolution and the rest migrated abroad. At present, there are less than fifteen Sikh families in Zahedan and about a hundred families in Tehran[19].

Gurdwaras built outside Afghanistan

The Gurdwaras in Afghanistan were also a community centre for the Sikhs. The Afghan Sikhs in New Delhi who migrated from different provinces have built Gurdwaras here to preserve their unique identity. They are as follows[20]:

1. Guru Nanak Darbar, Manohar Nagar – Jalalabad *Sangat*
2. Guru Arjan Dev Gurdwara, 47 Mahavir Road – Kabul *Sangat*
3. Guru Amar Das Gurdwara, 20 Block Tilak Nahar – Khost *Sangat*

4. Guru Tegh Bahadur Gurdwara – Helmand and Kandahar *Sangat*
5. Gurdwara Guru Ram Das – Helmand and Kandahar *Sangat*
6. Guru Har Rai Sahib Gurdwara, Near Dwarka Metro station – Kabul *Sangat*
7. Guru Angad Sahib Gurdwara, Karala – Khost *Sangat*
8. Gurdwara Guru Hargobind Sahib – Charikar (Parwan province) *Sangat.*

The Afghan Sikh community in Europe has built Gurdwaras in London, Stuttgart and Hamburg (both in Germany).

References

1. *Keshdhari* is a Sikh with uncut hair which includes beard and moustaches; the men also cover their head with a turban.
2. Ganda Singh. (1954). *Afghanistan da Safar*. New Delhi: Prakash & Co.
3. Those who do not keep uncut hair and are shaven but have full faith in the Sikh Gurus and the Guru Granth Sahib only.
4. The old name of Gurdwara. During the Guru Hargobind's time, the word Gurdwara became concurrent.
5. Khajinder S. Khurana. (2001). *Kabul de Sangat tee Afghanistan da Sankhep Ithas*. New Delhi.
6. The author spoke to an Afghan Hindu but was unable to secure his permission to share his name in the book.

7. As per the Sikh code of Conduct (*Rehat Maryada*), the Guru Granth Sahib is opened in the early morning (*Prakash*) and closed (*Sukh Aasan*) at night. *Nitnem, banis* and compositions are read in morning and evening.
8. Ischer Dass. (2003). *Die Gefahrten Afghanistans.* Berlin: IKO – Verlag für Interkulturelle Kommunikation.
9. Sweet dough made with equal portions of whole wheat flour, clarified butter and sugar. It is offered to all visitors to the Gurdwara.
10. Country Policy and Information Note-Afghanistan: Hindus and Sikhs, Home Office UK, Version 3.0 February 2017.
11. Information received on 18th August 2018 from Ram Saran Basin at Kabul.
12. Sangat Singh. (1994). *The Sikhs in History.* Amritsar: Singh Brothers.
13. *Mission Afghanistan* documentary.
14. Information provided by Ram Saran Basin from Kabul.
15. Confirmed by Kabul Sangat in June 2018.
16. This seems a very humble estimate in 1952. In 1973, Nancy Dupree states that there were 25,000–30,000 Sikhs and Hindus in the country. Khajinder Singh Khurana has stated that there were 60,000 Afghan Sikhs and Hindus (3:2 ratio) in 1992 just before they left the country. At present there could be about 100,000 Afghan Sikhs and Hindus across the globe.
17. The wounds of the 1947 partition riots were perhaps still fresh. In Pakistan, only the Sikhs are blamed for killing Muslims in East Punjab.

18. Zahedan was formerly known as Dozdab—*Dozd* for bandit, *Ab* for water. The literal meaning was a town of bandits by the water. It is said that when the Emperor, Reza Shah Pahlavi (1925–41) came to the town in the 1920s, he found Sikh men in white robes and flowing beards and asked what they were doing among the thieves. The Shah renamed the city as Zahedan which is the plural of the Arabic word *zahed* meaning 'pious'. https://www.ndtv.com/india-news/irans-connection-to-indias-sikhs-498087. Accessed on 10 February 2018.
19. Farideh Okati. (2014). 'The Sikh's Society in Zahedan and Their Multilingualism'. *Iranian Journal of Language Issues* (IJLI), vol. 1, no. 2.
20. Shamsher Singh and Khajinder S. Khurana, both are based in Delhi.

12

Building the Modern Afghanistan—20th Century

The 20th century saw the beginning of modernisation of Afghanistan and various rulers contributed to the development of the country. The role of the Afghan Sikhs and Hindus during this period is captured in this chapter.

Habibullah Khan (1901–19)

In 1903, Amir Habibullah Khan opened Habibia School, the first well-structured and modern school in Afghanistan. It served as the foundation for the country's education and training system. Most teachers of this school were either Afghans who were educated in India, or Muslim Indians who had arrived in Afghanistan due to political persecution. Dr Abdul Ghani, an Indian Muslim was the first principal of the school. By 1924, modern schools were opened in other parts of the country as well. Even a few Hindus successfully finished their education in these schools[1].

Many prominent Afghan personalities have graduated from this school including the current President Dr Ashraf Ghani and the former President Hamid

Karzai. The school was badly damaged during the 1990s and was renovated with the assistance of Government of India during December 2003–March 2006. The renovated school building was inaugurated jointly by President Hamid Karzai and Prime Minister of India Dr Manmohan Singh, on 28 August 2005. Since then, India has been assisting Habibia School by way of repair and maintenance, upgrading of labs, training of teachers, etc. In May 2016 the Government of India pledged $1 million over a ten-year period for the annual routine maintenance of Habibia High School in Kabul[2].

In 1911, the Amir decided to take care of the health sector and founded the first modern hospital in Afghanistan at Kabul. The doctors were from Turkey. The military hospital was located in the Sultanpur district. It was headed by a doctor from India. In the course of time, a number of hospitals were built throughout Afghanistan, but unfortunately, they were not enough[3]. In 1932, a medical faculty in Kabul was opened which later led to the medical wing of the University.

Ghobar mentions Meta Singh, a Frontier Afghan Sikh and owner of Kabul Café who remained in prison for thirteen years for refusing to spy for the British High Commission in Kabul. His wife, who was German, left Afghanistan[4]. This obviously happened before 1919.

Frederick Pollock (1940) writes that Habibullah was courteous in his dealings with the Hindus and Sikhs. The Amir was delighted to visit Lahore 'which had once been in the possession of his dynasty'. He also visited Harmandar Sahib (Golden Temple) in Amritsar and 'made friends with the Sikh priests'. He told the British official that he respected all religions but despised those (people) who were lukewarm in their own faith. Pollock adds that this act of 'toleration to their hereditary enemies (Sikhs) displeased the Afghan Sirdars' who also resented Habibullah's open friendliness with the British officials and their wives[5].

Amir Amanullah Khan (1919–29)

Following the declaration of Independence in 1919 and the short inconsequential war, the British and the Afghans started negotiations, initially in Rawalpindi and then in the hill town of Mussoorie, now in the Indian state of Uttarakhand. Dupree provides interesting details regarding the conference.

Nawab Sahibzada Abdul Qayyum Khan (a Muslim Pathan from Peshawar and a member of the British delegation) defended the British policy and Diwan Niranjan Das (an Afghan Hindu) defended the Afghan policy. The atmosphere in the town (and rest of the country) was pro-Afghan and there was a feeling of anticipation that following the Afghan independence, a similar process may start for India.

During the conference, *Eid al-Adha* occurred and given the violent atmosphere, the British initially refused the Afghan request to visit the mosque in Dehradun. Eventually, the British relented and Diwan Niranjan Das accompanied his Muslim colleagues to the mosque. The Afghan delegation also visited the famous Hindu pilgrimage at Hardwar 'to symbolize the ethnic unity which theoretically existed in Afghanistan'. Dupree writes that all along the route the local people kissed the car of the Afghan delegates and shouted independence slogans[6].

Article 2 of the Constitution of Afghanistan recognised minorities and it was approved in 1923. It stated:

> The religion of Afghanistan is the sacred religion of Islam. Followers of other religions such as Jews and Hindus residing in Afghanistan are entitled to the full protection of the state provided they do not disturb the public peace.

On 18th May 1925 during the reign of Amir Amanullah Khan, the Sikhs organised a three-day *Samagham* (religious programme) for the first time in the city of Kabul. The religious function was held in the garden of Diwan Niranjan Das' mansion. Giani Avtar Singh and Master Udham Singh were the main organisers. *Akhand Paathh,* the continuous recitation of the Guru Granth Sahib which is completed in forty-eight hours was undertaken. A *Nagar Kirtan,* a Sikh religious procession with the Guru Granth Sahib in a spacious vehicle which had the Khalsa flag and the flag of Afghanistan on either side was taken out in the city. On the last day, *Amrit Sanchar* (Khalsa initiation ceremony) for the willing was performed. The programme which was supported by the government was very well attended by the Afghan Sikhs and Hindus[7].

Ikbal Ali Shah (1938) mentions an interesting incident relating to a Sikh. Shah writes, 'In his Farman No. 55 he (Amir) writes to Mohammed Nadir Khan during the Afghan War that two motor-drivers, one Sikh and the other a Moslem, were brought before him, from whom he received valuable information of the English in India. He informs the General that these two most reliable informers are appointed to convey messages and news to the members of the Afghan Delegation in India'.

Shah rightly questions the amateur methods employed by Amir Amanullah Khan in procuring intelligence. He laments the level of corruption in the country and writes, 'there is even a better illustration of these unspeakable robberies when police officers kept regular gangs of thieves in their employ. First, the house of a merchant or well-to-do man was burgled, the spoils were, of course, divided amongst the members of the police; and, in the morning, arrests of other wealthy people of the town were made, who were released after bribes had been extorted from them. Sometimes appointments were sold for so much because they were to "yield" so much yearly'[8].

Amanullah removed most restrictions upon the Hindus and Shias in Afghanistan. Ghani (1921) writes that they could practice their religions as they liked and perform their rituals and other religious exercises. The Amir personally attended the religious functions of minorities. The *Jizya* on Hindus was reduced to half but the Hindus still had to wear a mark (*Kashka or tilak*) on the forehead which was 'ordered only for their safety'. Ghani writes that the former distinction of yellow turbans and caps for the Hindus was removed.

They had equal rights with the Muslims and were even taken in the military service. Ghani adds that in state service, the Muslims had no preference over the Hindus. He adds, 'Some of the highest posts in offices were occupied by Hindu gentlemen. The Hindus in Kabul mostly form the trading class but some of them learn clerical work and get engaged in offices on equal salaries with Mohammadans'[9].

The radio station and transmission were established during the reign of Amanullah Khan which was almost the same time as radio broadcasting started in British India. This was an achievement for modern Afghanistan.

The Amir favoured wearing western attires and etiquettes. He spoke against the *purdah* system and encouraged women's education. His wife Queen Soraya shed away the veil and started attending functions with her husband in public, in western outfits. Some girl students were sent to Turkey for higher education. The Queen became the face of women's rights in Afghanistan[10].

Dass writes that from 1923, Amir Amanullah Khan wanted to give Afghanistan a new impetus and begin economic and industrial growth. With the help of skilled people, he was able to start several schools, administrative structures, hospitals, and a few manufacturing companies. He travelled to Germany, France, Great Britain, Turkey and the then Soviet Union. When he came back, he wanted to change the life of the Afghan citizens. The rights of women were increased, and people were encouraged to wear western clothes and men were banned from wearing turbans. Although this was never strictly implemented beyond the city of Kabul, however, the conservatives thought that this was contrary to their religion. The fundamentalists highjacked the reforms of Amanullah Khan and began to resist and rebel over them. They succeeded in causing a religious and popular rage against the ruler. Although the economy was being modernised, the army outside Kabul was still rudimentary hence ill-prepared to crush the rebellion swiftly. The Amir decided to leave the country to avoid a civil war which would have led to the death of many Afghans. The Amir made far too many radical changes in the Afghan society in a short space of time like Ataturk of Turkey but unlike the latter, he did not succeed in embedding them in the Afghan culture.

Habibullah Kalakani—1929

During this period, Habibullah Bache Sakqau (the son of the water-bearer) from Kalakaan founded a group in the north of Kabul province, and after a few months was able to conquer the province of Kabul. He and his band were illiterate and rough headed and had no experience of running a government.

The Hindus and Sikhs, who lived in the province of Parwan, owned vineyards in Kalakaan and Charikar and had very friendly and neighbourly relations with the other villagers. They also had friendly relations with Habibullah Kalakani, as his father used to provide their drinking water. Kalakani was deposed after nine months[11].

Mohammed Nadir Shah (1929–33)

The first modern university in Afghanistan was the University of Kabul, which was opened in 1931 and included numerous faculties. It was followed by the University of Nangarhar, Kandahar University, University of Herat and the University of Balkh.

Higher education in Afghanistan lasted at least four years and a maximum of seven years. For the students, who came from other provinces to Kabul, a very good student dwelling, where girls and boys lived separately, was established. Like the apartments, the food and other amenities were financed by the government. Before 1978, all students also received a monthly allowance from the state[12].

In the course of time, collaborations were signed with countries such as Germany, France and the USA, which supported the educational institutions. This had brought numerous guest lecturers and professors into the country and the students were able to travel to Europe and the US for further studies. The former Soviet Union built the Kabul Polytechnic Institute in 1967 in over sixty hectares of land. In 2002 it became the Kabul Polytechnic University.

The educational attainment of the Afghan Sikhs and Hindus during this period was above the average level of education of the native population. Education like rest of the country suffered a lot during the Mujahideen and the Taliban regimes.

Zahir Shah (1933–73)

Traditionally, all the banking business in Afghanistan was in the hands of the Hindus (and Sikhs) and the Jewish money-lenders. In 1931, the first bank in the country was founded under the name of The National Bank of Afghanistan (*Shirkat-i-Ashami*) with branches at Herat, Kandahar, Mazar, Khanabad, Jalalabad, Peshawar, Bombay, London, Paris and Berlin. It was not a state-owned bank but had a monopoly over government business[13]. The first wholly government-owned bank was established in 1939 under the name of Da Afghanistan Bank (DAB).

Ahmad and Aziz (1936) write that all Afghans whether Aryan, Semitic or Turanian, Sunni, Shia or Hindu, are equally proud of their Afghan nationality and have even presented a united front to external foes.

In terms of minorities, Ahmad and Aziz add that the Jews were found in most towns north of the Hindukush and at Kabul while the Hindus and Sikhs were settled in all the towns and important villages[14].

During the reign of Zahir Shah, the government promoted pride in the pre-Islamic heritage of Afghanistan. Many books were published in the country and we are told that ancient Afghanistan was called 'Aryana', the land of Aryans. The national airline of the country was also named Aryana. Prof. Ganda Singh writes that many people were doing their PhDs on ancient Afghanistan and there was a lot of curiosity to learn about the pre-Islamic past of the country[15]. Foreign archaeology missions excavated and brought to light the Greek-Bactrian (Balkh), Buddhist Gandhara and the Hindu past of the country. The Pashtun identity and Pashto language were promoted. No one could fault the government of this except that although the Pashtun or Pakhtoon were considered synonymous with the Afghans, they were no more than 40 percent of the whole population. The Zahir Shah Government should have tried to be more inclusive.

During this period, the Hindus (and Sikhs) were considered as original inhabitants of Afghanistan and well respected. A Hindu gentleman from Kandahar mentions that the educated people quote the existence of various ancient temples as a proof of the Hindu presence in the country since antiquity, but the general masses think that Hindus were brought as slaves by Ahmed Shah Durrani[16].

Khurana has mentioned that some Sikhs and Hindus living in the border Frontier province (then called North West Frontier Province) crossed over to Afghanistan to escape the violence against them following the partition of British India into Pakistan and India. Khurana adds that many of them entered the Khost province in Afghanistan and continued to live there until 1992[17].

Prof. Ganda Singh in his *Diary of the Partition Days* quotes the English daily *Hindustan Times* dated 25th October 1947 which states as reported from Peshawar that a few thousand Hindus and Sikhs fled from Pakistan and have sought refuge in Kabul[18].

Dass provides the history of the cremation grounds in Kabul. A plot of 2,200 square metres was purchased by the Sikhs and Hindus in 1920 in Qalacha area outside the city of Kabul after seeking necessary permission. Thick walls which were two metres in height were built around the plot so that the cremations were done in private without disturbing anyone's sensibilities. At this time, the surrounding area was un-built. The two parts consisted of a building for the mourners in winters and a large yard with flowers and trees. The second part had the main firewood camp, the main cemetery and children's graveyard. Children under the age of seven were buried and those over seven years were cremated.

Dass writes that post-1992 when the Taliban were in power, the Sikhs cremated inside the Gurdwara Karte Parwan while the Hindus cremated in the front yard of the Asamai School[19]. The forty years of war and uncertainty has made the Afghans 'less tolerant and more fundamentalist' now. One of the biggest problems the Sikhs and Hindus now face is the cremation of their dead. The cremation grounds which were outside the Kabul city are now part of residential areas as the city has expanded. Now, whenever they try to cremate their dead, the local people throw stones and bricks at them. In the absence of any contingency plan, nowadays the community informs the police before coming to cremate their dead and the police provide them protection. Alas, gone are the days when some Afghans would consider Sikhs and Hindus as *Lala* or elder brother.

The period from 1960–80 was one of high achievement for the Afghan Sikhs and Hindus. The youth took immense interest in attaining higher education. During this time a number of doctors, engineers and other professionals came out of the community. In 1960, a joint Hindu-Sikh institution known as *Kharian* was formed. In 1965, the Sikh youth formed *'Naujawan Sikh Sabha'* for their social and religious requirements. The literal meaning is Sikh Youth Club/Organisation. Both organisations worked together in the field of education.

The members and organisers of these bodies were doctors and educated members of the community. They were in a mission to eradicate illiteracy and went to every house to encourage the community to study. They spoke in Gurdwaras and Mandirs on embracing modern education. In 1968, the *Afghan Sikh Sabha* was formed. It worked on gaining higher education and doing away with outdated social practices.

In 1969, the Vice-President of *Naujawan Sikh Sabha,* Jai Singh Faani won the election and became a Member of Parliament. This good work continued until 1978. During this time there was hardly any hospital in Jalalabad, Kabul and Kandahar which did not have a Sikh-Hindu doctor. The community also had professors in Universities of Kabul and Jalalabad. Some notable names were Professor Bal Mukand, Professor Saran Singh, Professor Bhagat Singh and Professor Roop Chand[20].

A new Constitution of Afghanistan was approved in 1964 which also reiterated the religious freedom of the minorities. The article 2 stated:

> Islam is the sacred religion of Afghanistan. Religious rites performed by the state shall be according to the provisions of the Hanafi doctrine. Non-Muslim citizens shall be free to perform their rituals within the limits determined by laws for public decency and public peace[21].

Prominent Sikhs and Hindus

The Afghan Sikhs and Hindus have historically worked as traders and lenders but many of them also became professionals. They played an important part in the Afghan society. Some of the eminent personalities were as follows:

Mangal Singh Bedi was the direct descendant of Guru Nanak Sahib, the first Guru of the Sikhs. It should be mentioned here that the Sikhs do not attach any importance to ancestry; however, if the descendant is a pious Sikh then the lineage is mentioned as a mark of respect.

He was born in Charikar and his father Jeet Singh was also a religious leader. He lived in Kabul and Kharikar and was very popular with everyone in Kalakaan, Charikar and Kabul, and everyone had much respect for him.

Mangal Singh participated in the *Loya Jirga* (Parliament) of 1925. In the year 1927, the Amir Amanullah Khan ordered his government and the honorary workers that any participant of the second *Loya Jirga* should not wear turbans. Basically, the Amir banned the turban but the proud Sikh who could not remove his turban due to religious reasons was denied membership of the *Loya Jirga*. His principles increased the prestige of Mangal Singh in the society[22].

Many government officials of Habibullah Kalakani attended the wedding of Mangal Singh in 1929. His relations with the subsequent kings, Nadir Shah and Zahir Shah were very cordial as well. He was affectionately known as Babaji. Following his death, his son Jagtar Singh took over the leadership role of the Sikhs.

Any book on Afghanistan usually tends to have a passing reference to the Afghan Sikhs. They tend to concentrate on the Sikhs' (of Punjab) engagement with Abdali and his successors. Ghobar mentions Baba Mangal Singh in some detail[23].

Ghobar seems to be unhappy with Mangal Singh's good relations with the Tajik usurper Habibullah Kalakani who took the throne of Kabul in 1929 for nine months. He calls Kalakani and his supporters, bandits. Ghobar writes that at the time of his wedding, Mangal Singh 'received an official entourage of cavalry and infantry to escort him to the house of his bride in Kalakan'. He calls Mangal Singh a mysterious man and wonders how he had good relations even with subsequent rulers. Needless to say, Mangal Singh was an enigmatic personality.

Diwan Niranjan Das[24] was born in 1867 in Kabul. He graduated from the Military School. Diwan Niranjan began with his career during the reign of King Habibullah Khan. When Amir Habibullah Khan appointed him to the 'Council of Nobility', he became famous[25].

Ischer Dass writes that when he attended sixth grade, his history teacher, Darwesh Khan, taught them that, in addition to the Muslims, Hindus had also participated in the liberation struggle (against British). Diwan Niranjan Das headed the Afghan delegation, which travelled to India in July 1920 and signed the charter of Afghanistan's freedom from the British Empire.

Amir Amanullah Khan appointed Diwan Niranjan as the state Minister of Finance and Trade in his Government. For the next few years, he actively participated in all diplomatic efforts. As he had finished military school, Diwan always wore a military uniform and was armed with a sword.

Diwan had only one child, a daughter Radha affectionately called Radojaan. She was very beautiful but such was the status of Diwan Niranjan Das that none of Hindus dared to ask her hand in marriage. The Diwan went to India where she was married off.

Khurana quotes the Diwan's granddaughter Subadra Bali who was about 90–92 years of age when he met her. She told Khurana that Diwan, like the other Afghan Hindus, was very close to the Sikhs. He regularly visited Gurdwara Baba Sri Chand to pay his respects. In 1920, the Diwan for the first time took a *Jatha* (group) of Afghan Sikhs and Hindus to India and visited various Sikh and Hindu places of worship in India. The *Jatha* filled about fifteen to twenty coaches of the train in Peshawar. The *Jatha* visited Panja Sahib, Nankana Sahib,

Dera Sahib (Lahore), Darbar Sahib (Amritsar), Badrinath, Haridwar and Ayodhya.

In 1923, Amir Amanullah Khan voluntarily surrendered power and fled to Italy in order to avoid a civil war. The singers made folklore songs on the Diwan and his daughter as the former was a key minister of the Amir.

0 Dochtare Diwaan, Bibi Radojaan

Oh daughter of Diwan, dear Ms Rado

Lalla ra Qasam dadom, ke rado ra nazozaan

I requested *Lala* (could be her father or any other Hindu in her family such as brother) do not cremate Rado (after her death).

Diwan Niranjan Das died at the age of sixty-five in 1932. His brother, Diwan Sadhu Ram was the deputy Governor of Kandahar.

Another prominent Afghan Sikh personality was Giani Nihal Singh 'Afeef'. According to Khurana he was born in Bannu (NWFP) and following the partition of British India in 1947, he went to Kabul and lived there for twenty years where he taught English, Gurmukhi and Farsi to students. He wrote many books but is especially remembered for translating the *Japji Sahib* and *Sukhmani Sahib* (compositions from Guru Granth Sahib) into Farsi. He had also translated a major portion (if not all) of the Guru Granth Sahib but it was lost in the anti-Sikh carnage in Delhi in 1984.

The Farsi translation of *Japji* and *Sukhmani Sahib* were published under the names of *Nagmeh Urfan* and

Gahwahre Rahat respectively. Mohd Khan Zakariya, the former Afghan minister wrote that these writings were spiritual and tender and would be remembered in future as a milestone of its time.

Jai Singh 'Faani' has been described by Khurana as an accomplished and multi-personality Afghan Sikh. He was a successful businessman and social activist. Faani started the *Naujawan Sikh Sabha* (Sikh Youth Club) in 1965. He was an excellent orator and proficient in Punjabi, Farsi, Urdu, Pashto, Hindi and English. Whoever listened to him could not help but be impressed. In 1969, at the age of twenty-eight, he was elected to the Parliament as an independent candidate. He won many hearts with his passionate speeches in the Parliament and by his work among the rich and poor of Kabul. Faani's honesty and integrity won him admirers across all parties. In 1973, in a bloodless coup, Zahir Shah was deposed and his first cousin Daoud Khan declared Afghanistan a Republic and proclaimed himself as its first President. The new President invited Faani to join his cabinet which the latter politely declined. After much persuasion, Faani relented in 1977 and was going to join the Finance ministry, but destiny had something else stored for him. He took ill on 19th April and on 25th April 1977 he boarded a plane to New Delhi for treatment when he died during the journey. A year later on 28th April 1978, President Daoud Khan was assassinated and Afghanistan plunged into unrest and war which unfortunately since then has never ended. In 1992, in recognition of his service to the Afghan Sikh community, his photograph was added to the

Central Sikh Museum in the Harmandar Sahib (Golden Temple), Amritsar.

Sikhs and Hindus—1970s[26]

Louis Dupree in his book *Afghanistan* published in 1973 mentions Sikhs and Hindus in Afghanistan. He writes that the 1964 constitution guarantees freedom of worship to non-Muslims 'within the limits determined by law, decency and public peace' (Article 2, paragraph 2). He mentions that the only non-Muslim member in *Loya Jirga,* a Hindu from Kabul 'expressed satisfaction with this article but hoped that laws concerning minority groups would keep the spirit of the Constitution'.

Dupree writes that the majority of the 30,000 Sikhs and Hindus were merchants in cities and towns and wrote in the Arabic script of Western Punjabi dialects. Later, there is a slight contradiction when he states that there are 25,000 of them, who were Afghan nationals and 200 Indian nationals as per 'their own estimates'[27].

Dupree writes that Sikhs 'constitute the majority (about 15,000) of Afghan nationals of Indian origin'. He adds that the Sikhs (and Hindus) primarily engaged in commercial activities and there were few towns in Afghanistan 'without their quota of Hindu and Sikh businessmen'. The Sikhs generally exhibited the 5Ks in a 'somewhat modified form' and wore miniature silver kirpan around their necks. Dupree confuses the *kada,* the iron bangle in the wrist which is one of the 5Ks as a miniature version of *chakar* (steel quoit worn on the turban) which is sometimes still worn by

Nihang Singhs and Sikhs in Indian Army but is not obligatory for Sikhs.

Dupree acknowledges the Hindus in ancient Afghanistan and writes that 'Historically, the Hindus played an important role in shaping the destiny of Afghanistan especially in the eastern and southern areas'. He mentions the Mauryan, Gupta and Hindu Shahi dynasties and writes that some Afghan Hindus claimed the Hindu Shahi ancestry. But despite this acknowledgement, Dupree refers to the Hindus and Sikhs as two groups of Indian origin.

The Hindus and Sikhs actively practiced their respective religions and maintained their distinctive places of worship. Dupree adds most still spoke Hindi or Punjabi. He mentions of discrimination, 'Indian nationals operate under an Afghan-Indian barter agreement. Afghan nationals of Indian extraction, however, work under Afghan laws and sometimes suffer discrimination of varying degrees in government offices'. However, the Sikh and Hindu young men performed national service and while on active duty, the Sikhs were permitted to wear the five Ks.

The Afghan economy

Mohammed Ali (1958) mentions an intriguing point about the discovery of the sea route between Europe and South Asia in 1498 which affected the prosperity of medieval Afghanistan. According to him, prior to this discovery, the cities of Balkh, Bukhara and Samarkand were part of the famous Silk Route and were very prosperous[28]. However, until the late 18th century, Afghanistan had seaports by virtue of being part of Persia and Mughal India. In early and mid-18th century the Hotak and Durranis established a big Empire and had seaports. It was only during the reign of Timur Durrani (1772–93) that it became landlocked. Nevertheless, the British writers from the 19th century note traders and merchants doing a brisk business in the country.

The Suez Canal was formally opened in 1869 and it reduced the distance between the Indian Ocean and the Mediterranean Sea by almost 7,000 km. Afghanistan could not avail any benefits from it but neither did most of Asia and Africa as they were colonies of European powers. However, there is some truth that being a landlocked country has been disadvantageous to Afghanistan. It has to rely on either of its two neighbouring countries to act as a transit for import and export of goods. Even during the relatively peaceful era of Zahir Shah (1933–73), the country was far from being self-reliant and was dependent on foreign aid. In present times, in the absence of Pakistan's consent, India has been sending its exports to Iran from where they are then sent to Afghanistan over land.

References

1. Ischer Dass. (2003). *Die Gefahrten Afghanistans*. Berlin: IKO.
2. https://www.khaama.com/india-pledges-1-million-for-habibia-high-school-in-kabul-01014/. Accessed on 9th July 2018.

3. Ischer Dass. (2003). *Die Gefahrten Afghanistans*. Berlin: IKO.
4. Mir Gholam Mohammad Ghobar. (2001). *Afghanistan in the Course of History: Vol 2,* (translated by Sherief A Fayez). The first volume was published in 1967. The remaining chapters were translated and published as Volume 2 in 2001.
5. Frederick Pollock. (1940). *A History of Afghanistan*. London: Macmillan & Co.
6. Louis Dupree. (1973). *Afghanistan,* New York: Princeton University Press.
7. Khajinder Singh Khurana. (2001). *Kabul di Sikh Sangat tee Afghanistan da Sankhep Ithas*. New Delhi.
8. Sirdar Ikbal Ali Shah. (1938). *Modern Afghanistan*. London: Sampson Low.
9. Abdul Ghani, (1921). *A Review of the Political Situation in Central Asia,* Lahore: Khosla Brothers.
10. Huma Ahmed-Ghosh. (2003). 'A History of Women in Afghanistan: Lessons Learnt for the Future or Yesterdays and Tomorrow'. *Journal of International Women's Studies*. Vol 4, no. 3, pp. 1–14.
11. Khajinder Singh Khurana. (2001). *Kabul di Sikh Sangat tee Afghanistan da Sankhep Ithas*. New Delhi.
12. Ischer Dass. (2003). *Die Gefahrten Afghanistans*. Berlin: IKO.
13. Sirdar Ikbal Ali Shah. (1938). *Modern Afghanistan*. University of Michigan.
14. Jamaluddin Ahmad and Mohd Abdul Aziz. (1936). *Afghanistan—A Brief Survey*. London: Longman Green & Co.
15. Ganda Singh. (1954). *Afghanistan da Safar*. New Delhi: Parkash and Co.

16. After the last week of May 2018, the Afghan Hindu source developed cold feet and did not speak again to the author, perhaps due to fear of repercussion for speaking out of turn. The author could not seek his permission to use his name in the book.
17. Khajinder Singh Khurana. (2001). *Kabul di Sikh Sangat tee Afghanistan da Sankhep Ithas*. New Delhi.
18. Ganda Singh. (1960). 'A Diary of the Partition Days'. *Journal of Indian History. Vol XXXVIII Part I,* no. 112. April 1960.
19. Ischer Dass. (2003). *Die Gefahrten Afghanistans*. Berlin: IKO.
20. Khajinder Singh Khurana. (2001). *Kabul di Sikh Sangat tee Afghanistan da Sankhep Ithas*. New Delhi.
21. Louis Dupree. (1973). *Afghanistan*. New York: Princeton University Press.
22. Khajinder Singh Khurana. (2001). *Kabul di Sikh Sangat tee Afghanistan da Sankhep Ithas*. New Delhi.
23. Mir Gholam Mohammad Ghobar. (2001). *Afghanistan in the Course of History. Vol* 2 (translated by Sherief A Fayez).
24. The Diwan was from a Mohyal Brahmin family. Khurana writes that he regularly visited Gurdwara Baba Sri Chand in Kabul. The Afghan Hindus were very close to the Sikh religion and would read and recite the Gurbani (compositions from the Guru Granth Sahib).
25. Ischer Dass. (2003). *Die Gefahrten Afghanistans*. Berlin: IKO.
26. Louis Dupree. (1973). *Afghanistan*. New York: Princeton University Press.

27. This seems a very low estimate unless within twenty years the Hindus and Sikhs had doubled. Khurana mentions 60,000 Sikhs and Hindus before 1992.
28. Mohammed Ali. (1958). *Afghanistan The National Awakening*. Lahore: Punjab Educational Press.

13

Sahajdhari Sikhs and Dual Belief Hindus

The *Encyclopaedia of Sikhism* (by Dr Harbans Singh) under the *Sahajdhari* entry describes them as 'a gradualist among Sikhs'. Like other Sikhs, the *Sahajdharis* believe in the ten Sikh Gurus and in the Guru Granth Sahib but exempt themselves from the obligation of keeping their hair unshorn (and wearing a turban). Most *Sahajdharis* will not have the Sikh surname of 'Singh'[1].

The word *Sahaj* (in Sanskrit, *Sahaja*) implies poise, unhurriedness and the word *dhari* stands for adopting or accepting a creed or form. Harbans Singh states that this term came into use after Guru Gobind Singh initiated the Khalsa in 1699 CE, introducing the *Khande di Pahul,* that is baptism by the double-edged sword. Those who took *Khande di Pahul* received the title of the Khalsa and those who for one reason or another could not are known as *Sahajdharis*. The other name for *Sahajdhari* was *Nanakpanthi* as noted in the book, *Dabistan-i-Mazahib*. The ultimate ideal is to take '*Amrit*' and become Khalsa. Some *Sahajdhari* parents take a bow to raise their firstborn son as a Khalsa.

As the *Sangat* was in far-flung areas including Afghanistan and the Frontier province it was not possible to administer *Khande di Pahul* in the first instance. The ongoing conflict with the Mughals became another obstacle but the *Sahajdhari* families provide at least one of their sons to become Khalsa. Harbans Singh writes that the *Sahajdharis* have been part of the larger Sikh body since the time of Guru Gobind Singh and names contemporaries Ghazni-born Persian scholar, Bhai Nand Lal and Bhai Kanhaiya, the great humanitarian who were *Sahajdharis* and were held in great esteem by Sikhs.

During the early part of the 18th century, the Sikhs faced extreme persecution and anyone with long hair and turban faced instant death. The *Sahajdhari* looked after the places of worship and protected the household while the Khalsa continued the struggle through guerrilla warfare while living in hills and jungles. Teenager Haqiqat Rai who was accused of insulting Islam, preferred death instead of accepting Islam; Diwan Kaura Mall, minister under the Mughal governor Muin ul Mulk (1738–53) helped Sikhs in many ways and Des Raj who was entrusted with the task of the reconstruction of Harmandar Sahib in Amritsar (following demolishment by Ahmed Shah Abdali in 1762) were *Sahajdharis*.

Diwan Dinanath who was the Finance Minister and Bhai Vasti Ram, a learned man well versed in the Sikh scripture were both *Sahajdharis* and enjoyed considerable influence at the court of Maharaja Ranjit Singh (1799–1839).

Harbans Singh notes that the *Sahajdharis* associated themselves with the Sikh-run institutions and organisations such as the *Shiromani Gurdwara Parbandhak Committee, Chief Khalsa Diwan, Shiromani Akali Dal,* and the *All India Sikh Students Federation*. The *Singh Sabhas* (local Gurdwaras) used to have seats on their executive committees reserved for the *Sahajdharis*. In addition, prior to 1947, they had their own societies namely *Sahajdhari Committee of Multan, Guru Nanak Sahajdhari Diwan* of Panja Sahib and *Sri Guru Nanak Sahajdhari Jatha* of Campbellpore (Attock, West Punjab).

The population of *Sahajdhari* Sikhs in Punjab reduced from 20 percent in 1891 to 6.5 percent (282,000) in 1931 of the total Sikh population. There was a corresponding increase in the number of *Keshdhari* Sikhs[2].

Dual Beliefs of Afghan Hindus

The Hindus and Sikhs had a very close relation in Afghanistan. They were a minuscule minority (1% or even less) in a conservative Muslim country. They used to visit each other's places of worship in happiness and sadness. Some Hindus also revered the Sikh Gurus and recited the *Gurbani,* compositions from the Guru Granth Sahib.

The *Sahajdhari* Sikhs are known as *Sevaks* in Afghanistan. The word *Seva* means voluntary service and the person doing it is called a *Sevak*. Due to their profound reverence and *Seva* at Gurdwaras these people came to be known as *Sevak* (of the Guru). However, the root of this word is *Sevok* which in Persian means

Mona or shaven. The *Sevak* believed in all the tenets of the Sikh religion but did not have unshaven hair, beard and the 5Ks of Khalsa. Many of these *Sevaks* became Khalsa when the Sikh doctrine was preached among them in the 20th century.

The community from Khost province is of *Sahajdhari* Sikhs. They are Pashto speaking 'shaven' Sikhs. Dr Anarkali Honaryar, the first Afghan non-Muslim woman parliamentarian is from the Khost community. This community has built two Gurdwaras in New Delhi. In July 2018, the Khost community from Kabul came to their ancestral province to repair the Gurdwara which was hit by a rocket-missile in December 1992 in retaliation to the demolition of the disputed Babri Masjid in Ayodhya, India. Many Gurdwaras and Mandirs were attacked all across Afghanistan after the demolition in India. This (repair of Gurdwara) was also a symbolic gesture of defiance after the devastating suicide bomber attack on Sikhs and Hindus in Jalalabad on 1st July which left nineteen dead and killed almost the entire leadership of the Afghan Sikhs and Hindus.

Shamsher Singh, an Afghan Sikh in his late twenties, who emigrated to India in late 2016 from Lashkargah (Helmand province) provides related information. He informs that his late father was a *Sahajdhari* Sikh and well conversant in *Gurbani* and would do *Seva* in the local Gurdwara. All four sons were taught Sikh tenets and Gurmukhi. Shamsher started growing his hair and became *Keshdhari* in 2010 and took *Khande di Pahul* and became a Khalsa in 2012. He married a Khalsa girl and his son is being raised as a Khalsa-Sikh. Two of his other brothers are also Khalsa-Sikhs. All the brothers reside in New Delhi now including the one who is still *Sahajdhari* and they continue to be close to each other.

Surnames and Castes

A vast majority of the Sikhs and Hindus belong to the Arora and Khatri caste, now associated with the trading class. Khatri is a Punjabi variant of Kshatriya, the second caste under the *Varna* system. Some of the Afghan Hindu surnames are Arenja, Channa, Gandhi, Kapoor, Chugh, Gawdi, Narang, Adi[3], Jagga, Makkad, Gawri, Kukreja, Soni, Chopra, Virmani, Kakkar, Talwar, Mehra, Sharma, Gusain (Goswami), Chopra, Dhawan, Sarai[4].

The popular Sikh surnames are Sethi, Batra, Gurwara (Grover), Madaan, Sapra, Dhingra, Khurana, Handa, Vohra, Kapoor, Chawla, Kakarm Gaba, Bewas, Wadhwa, Arora, Chugh, Gulati, Matta, Longani, Soni, Malhotra, Dang, Babbar (found in Ghazni), Bhatia[5].

Future

The number of Afghan Sikhs exceeds that of Afghan Hindus. Nancy Dupree puts it in the ratio 3:2 (60–40%). Some Afghan Hindus (not *Sahajdhari*) read and recited *Gurbani* but also held Hindu Gods and Goddesses in reverence and celebrated Hindu festivals. In addition, some may also follow the *Radha Swami Sect* (which follows the *Bani* of Guru Granth Sahib) and various Babas (self-proclaimed religious heads)[6]. These Afghan Hindus with dual beliefs are similar to Hindus in North

Sindh, Baluchistan and Khyber Pakhtunkhwa provinces in Pakistan[7].

The Afghan Sikhs and Hindus lived in a mutually dependent relationship as the Afghan society (like most of India) was close-knit where neighbours were the first protocol for help and assistance. In the UK and Germany (and other Western countries) the local government fills that gap. Life is busy in these countries and the Afghan Sikhs and Hindus have established their own Gurdwaras and Mandirs but could be influenced by the larger communities of Punjabi Sikhs and Hindus. At present, the Afghan Hindus are trying to adhere to their tradition. The Asamai temples have been built in various countries in Europe and North America. The temples in London and Germany ask the devotees to cover their heads in the temple. This is strictly implemented. The religious programme ends with an *Ardas*[8], a clear influence of Sikh religion.

However, when these people from dual beliefs come to India or Western English-speaking countries where Sikhs and Hindus are in appreciable numbers their dual beliefs are questioned. As they do not wear a turban (and do not have a beard and long hair) and their names do not have *Singh* in them, they are asked why they recite the *Gurbani*. The next generation starts associating themselves with Hindus but some continue to have reverence for the Sikh religion. The Sindhi Hindus in India who migrated from Sindh to mainland India in 1948 are a good example. There is a section among them who are very close to the Sikh tenets but in the census, they will state their religion as Hinduism. However, if a *Keshdhari* Sikh (out of ignorance) tells a *Sevak* or *Sehajdhari* that they are not Sikhs that would offend them.

Their new generation especially based outside East Punjab does not learn the Gurmukhi script which makes them unable to read *Gurbani* (although it is available in other scripts as well). The Sikh community of whom three-fourths are Punjabi, do not reach out to these people[9]. Within a couple of generations most of them leave their 'Sikh beliefs' and become 'more Hindu' to fit in with the Hindu majority in India. The Afghan Hindu community, if not all may be heading in this direction in India and abroad.

On a positive note, although compared to Afghanistan, the Afghan Sikhs and Hindus in Europe are less close due to multiple factors discussed above but the new generation is studying in schools and colleges with different ethnicities and has developed a friendship with them. Hence in some ways, different communities are coming closer and becoming a part of the global village. London-based Afghan Sikh, Pritpal Singh, launched his second documentary, *Hindu Kush to Thames* in 2015 which beautifully explores the lives and challenges facing the Afghan Sikhs and Hindus who are now settled in London[10].

References

1. Harbans Singh. (1992). *Encyclopaedia of Sikhism*. Patiala: Punjabi University.

2. Harbans Singh. (1992). *Encyclopaedia of Sikhism*. Patiala: Punjabi University.
3. Information provided by Anil Arora from Germany.
4. Chander Kumar Sharma, London. The author spoke to Dr Madan Lal Shikarpuri, an Afghan Hindu in London who was a physician in Kabul. His real surname was Kapoor and informed that he has a record of his family from the last 300 years in Afghanistan and traces his family roots for about 900 years earlier. Another Afghan Hindu in the USA stated that his ancestors came from Multan and his surname was Khanna. Both these surnames are considered Punjabi of Khatri caste. The migration of Multani traders to Shikarpur in the late 17th century has been recorded by Sindhi historians.
5. Pritpal Singh, London and Shamsher Singh, New Delhi.
6. Confirmed from several sources across the globe.
7. Covered in other chapters of this book.
8. *Ardas* is a supplication addressed to the Almighty with folded hands. It is said after reciting the daily *banis* (prayers), completion of *keertan* (hymn-singing) or any other religious programme. Sometimes it is performed to seek divine assistance before undertaking a significant task.
9. A Sindhi Hindu in his twenties from Nasik, Maharashtra laments that mainstream Sikhs have not preached the gospel of Guru Nanak and due to this, Sindhi Hindus are attracted to Radha Swami sect which follows the *Bani* of Guru Granth Sahib but has a 'living Guru'. The mainstream Sikhs are against the concept of 'living Guru' as it is against the tenants of Sikh religion.

10. First documentary, *Mission Afghanistan* was launched in early 2013. Further details in the chapter titled 'Present Status and Future'.

14

Mandirs in Afghanistan

Ischer Dass, an Afghan Hindu settled in Germany wrote *Die Gefahrten Afghanistans* in 2003 in German. Khajinder Singh Khurana, an Afghan Sikh now living in New Delhi has written the book *Kabul di Sikh Sangat tee Afghanistan da Sankhep Ithas* (The Sikh Sangat of Kabul and Brief History of Afghanistan) in Punjabi language in 2001. Both these valuable books provide several details about the history of Mandirs in Afghanistan.

The Afghans have been very close to their faith and this also includes the Afghan Sikhs and Hindus. Ischer Dass interestingly writes that in the 1970s, Afghanistan became very liberal and during this period most of the temples and Gurdwaras were rebuilt. The Hindus and the Sikhs contributed from their pockets for this venture. The electric cables were modernised and the best building blocks, marble and carpets were used.

Dass writes that in Afghanistan the mosques get free water, electricity and are not subject to taxation. However, this benefit was not extended to temples and Gurdwaras. They were registered in the name of certain people and hence deemed as private property who had to pay for the utilities and appropriate taxes.

Temples in Kabul

Asamai Mandir, according to the western writers is the temple of the 'Lady of Hope'. The word *Asah* (or Asha) means hope and *Mai* means Lady. Dass writes that the history of this temple is as old as the history of Afghanistan. The temple was located in the cave at Asamai Mountain. The Pandava brothers (of *Mahabharata*) are said to have visited and worshipped at this place.

The Hindus would go up the mountain especially during the *Navratri* (literally, nine nights) festival week and come down again after praying. Amir Abdul Rahman Khan (reign 1880–1901) granted permission to build a temple on the lower side of the mountain. Khurana writes that the Amir sent a *palki* (palanquin) for the idol and building materials. The new temple had a rivulet next to it and when the idol would be bathed in milk, it would get mixed with the water downhill and look like a stream of milk. This place also came to be known as Zu-e-Sheer (stream of milk).

The present Afghan Hindus inform that in 1973, with the assistance of the Japanese, the government installed a television tower on the mountain. The Afghan Hindu and Sikh community pleaded that a tower should not be installed at the site as it had an ancient idol of Goddess Asamai and that the Hindus visited it frequently, especially during the *Navratri* festival. The Government deemed it as a suitable place for the tower as it is one of the highest points in Kabul, therefore, the objections by the Afghan Hindu-Sikh community were ignored. The transmitter was installed in mid-1978. The Hindus now had to share the place with a TV tower and transmitter much to their disappointment.

Dass writes that in 1982 the front building of the Asamai temple (lower side of the mountain) with a double storey and basement was built. Every year during the festival of Diwali, high government officials join the ceremonies and celebrations. Special prayers are held every Tuesday and Friday.

In 2006, a Mandir was constructed at the hilltop and was funded by Ehsan Bayat, an Afghan Muslim and founder of the Bayat Foundation, a charity which works for water projects and better healthcare and education for Afghan women and families.

Yogi Rattan, a *Nath Panth* ascetic that follows Gorakhnath's monastic order came to Kabul from India and spent the last few years of his life in the city. The Dargah Peer Rattan Nath Mandir is dedicated to him. The temple is located in Jada Maiwand area of Kabul and according to Dass, it was built during the rule of Timur Shah (reign 1772–93). Dass adds that prior to this structure there was a small, old temple here from the seventh or eighth century. Yogi Rattan Nath came and started preaching at this ancient temple. A complaint was made to the ruler that a Hindu is preaching and the Yogi proved his mettle by performing a miracle.

Khurana states that the Dargah is about 840 years old. Like Gorakhnath, there is little consensus among historians regarding the lifespan of Rattan Nath. There is a Dargah Mandir in his name in Ghazni, Jalalabad,

Peshawar, New Delhi and other places in India. In Bathinda (East Punjab), he is known as Haji Pir Rattan Nath, a Muslim! However, there is a general consensus that he passed away in Kabul.

Dass informs that the temple was completely rebuilt in 1970. In addition to morning prayers, Hindus regularly worship here on Tuesdays and Fridays. We are told that there is a tradition where once a year goat meat is cooked with rice and distributed to the worshippers. The temple is also known as Baba Har Shri Nath Mandir and Jhandewala Mandir (*jhanda* means flag). The Afghan Hindus greet each other with the usual salutation 'Ram Ram' and 'Har Shri Nath'.

In addition, there is Bhairo Mandir in Shor Bazaar which is a functional Mandir. A Hindu family lives there. This Mandir is next to the Bhai Mansa Singh Gurdwara. A few Mandirs in the city like the Hanuman Mandir were abandoned and they were occupied by the neighbours from the majority community[1].

Jalalabad

Khurana mentions that Sheva near Jalalabad has a place dedicated to the Hindu God Shiva. It is alleged that this is illegally occupied by miscreants from the majority community. Near it, a place in Darai Nur district has a stream which is known as RamKund. One side of the stream has hot and the other side has cold water. Devotees come and bathe in the stream.

Dargah Mathura Das in Jalalabad, according to Ischer Dass was built during the reign of Sher Shah Suri

(1538–45) in Jalalabad. Mathra (or Mathura) Das was the tenth Nath 'Guru' of Nath Panth. This religious Yogi order, Nath Panth, was founded by Gorakh Nath.

Mathura Das emigrated from India to Afghanistan. He chose Sultanpur (near Jalalabad) as his new home and started giving sermons. He built a prayer house about thirty square metres large which had four gates. After his death, a tomb was built here. In 1971, the Hindu community erected a new building by replacing the old structure. After the Dargah Peer Rattan Nath and the Asamai Temple in Kabul, this is the third largest Hindu temple in Afghanistan. The fundamentalists destroyed and burnt the temple Dargah Mathura Dass in Jalalabad on 7th September 1992. Following the defeat of the Taliban, it has been rebuilt.

Saathi in his book has written in some detail about the Hindus in Jalalabad. Most of the Hindus in the city had surnames like Lund, Kakar, Sachdev, Sehgal, Ahuja, Khanna and Puri. The Dargah Mandir had a big hall with a stage where the *Ramayana,* the Geeta and the *Simritis* (holy books) were placed and read to the congregation (prior to the exodus). The Hindus celebrated a number of festivals namely *Krishna Janamashtami, Ram Navami, Eka Darshi, Shivratri,* Holi, Diwali, Lohri, *Puranmashi, Navratri, Rakhi, Bhaiya Dooj, Karva Chauth* and Tuesday fasting among others. The congregation would gather on Tuesdays and Sundays. The *prasad* was given to the devotees. Occasionally, a *bhandara* was organised. Gosain Manmohan Das, the main organiser is commended in the book for implementing a number of improvements and the astute running of the Mandir.

Saathi has shared a very interesting incident regarding the Sikhs and Hindus in Jalalabad. In February 1954, the local authorities at Jalalabad called in the Sikh leaders and communicated the government's decision on the modernisation plan for Jalalabad which involved extending and enlarging the road network. The Gurdwara had come under the plan and the Sikhs were asked to vacate the premises so that it could be demolished to make way for the new road. The Sikhs were given land in the garden of Dargah Mandir to build their place of worship. The Sikhs protested and served prison terms for it, but the authorities did not budge. With no option left the Sikhs started building the Gurdwara in the garden. However, the Hindus objected when the Sikhs took a decision to cut the existing Peepal trees which the former considered as scared. Without cutting the trees the Gurdwara building could not be extended. This resulted in rare clashes between a section of Sikhs and Hindus. This was reported to seniors of the community who approached their peers in Kabul. The Hindus and Sikhs of Jalalabad and Kabul made a joint petition to the Emperor and requested that the Gurdwara should be handed back to the Sikhs as this issue was causing discontent among Hindus and Sikhs which was not in the best interest of the country (these communities were into money lending, local banking and business). Emperor Zahir Shah patiently listened to them and issued a royal edict and the Gurdwara was handed back to the Sikhs. The transport plan was changed, and the new road did not touch the Gurdwara[2].

Zabul

Mandir Shiv Bhulaan in Qalati Ghiliji is an ancient temple located near Qalati Ghiliji or simply Qalat which is the capital of Zabul province in Southern Afghanistan.

Khurana writes that one must go on their knees to reach this place. The place has idols of the Hindu God Shiva. In absence of any light in the cave-temple, devotees carry a torch with them. There is a stream of water where devotees take bath.

Hadden uses the name Ghar Bolan Baba for this temple and states that it is at an altitude of 1,795 metres. He adds that the cave was beautiful with natural rock formations and was used by the Hindus as a place of worship. We are told that the Hindus coloured the stalagmites (conical pillar rising from the cave floor) in red and yellow[3].

Ghazni

Khurana mentions an ancient cave temple on a hill in a Dargah near Ghazni which is still visited by the Hindu devotees. Qarabagh district has an ancient temple dedicated to a Goddess. It is said that there was a 'stream of milk' nearby but not anymore. It may have dried up. This place is also known as Sheer (milk in Dari language). Qarabagh also has well known Buddhist caves.

The Hindus had left the keys of Dargah Peer Rattan Nath Mandir in Ghazni with the Sikhs who cleaned it once a week, put on a *jot/deva* (a traditional lamp made of clay, with a cotton wick which is burned in ghee or vegetable oil) on Tuesday[4]. Latest information received states that there is a Hindu priest now looking after this Mandir[5].

Kandahar

Prior to 1992, there were over 5,000 Hindus in Kandahar and there were at least fourteen temples[3]. Now, the number of Hindus is less than ten. Like most of the country, these individuals now stay in a Gurdwara in Kandahar due to lack of housing. In addition, most if not all temples are occupied by miscreants from the majority community.

Despite best efforts, there is scarce information about the Hindu temples in Kandahar. A number of Afghan Hindus developed cold feet when revealed that the information provided by them would be included in a book. The fear of giving wrong information along with the fact that the author to them was an unknown entity deterred them. Although it was not stated explicitly, there seems to be a general fear among locals not to 'rock the boat'.

However, the existence of the following temples was confirmed as stated in Ischer Dass' book:

1. Hanuman Mandir, in the Shikarpuri Darwaza area
2. Narsinh Dwara, Shikarpuri Bazar
3. Lalji Dwara, Shikarpuri Bazar
4. Shamji Dwara, Shikarpuri Bazar

5. Hanuman Mandir, Kabuli Bazar
6. Shivala (Shiv Mandir), Kabuli Bazar
7. Devi Mandir (Dwara), Kabuli Bazar
8. Thakur Dwara, Kabuli Bazar (or Shikarpuri Bazar)
9. Shiv (Mandir) Dwara, Kabuli Bazar
10. Bhola Nath Mari, Kabuli Bazar
11. Shiv Lal Mari (Samadhi), Kabuli Bazar
12. Devi Dwara, out of the city of Kandahar (near Dand)
13. Jham Peer Sahib, (near Sarpooza) district Kandahar
14. Thaan Sahib, Shikarpuri Bazar.

Devi Dwara outside Kandahar city in the district is dedicated to the Goddess Durga. There is a Shivala Mandir nearby as well. These two places of worship are informed to be under the Hindus. In their vicinity, are the famous Chehel Dokhtaran hills.

Chehel means forty and *Dokhtaran* means girls. During the reign of Amir Abdur Rahman (1880–1901), any rebellion was brutally suppressed. He led many campaigns against the Hazaras who are of Shia Muslim faith and have partial Mongolian features (especially the eyes) which make them easily recognisable. They face a lot of discrimination in Afghanistan. In one such campaign, it is said that forty young Hazara women were resisting the troops but when cornered at the top of Shashpar Mountains, they jumped from the top and died rather than getting arrested and risk violation of their dignity and modesty. The mountains were covered with blood and were later named Chehel Dokhtaran.

Update from Kandahar[6]

The Hanuman Mandir was a temple in one room of a private household. They had made a Mandir inside and the family lived in rest of the house. They left the country about six or seven years ago and sold off the property. Hence, this Mandir does not exist now.

Narsingh Dwara had a Krishna Mandir as well. It also had a school up to the sixth standard and in addition, the students were taught Gurmukhi and Hindi.

The last report received from Kandahar states that there are five Hindus and four Sikhs in Kandahar. They live in one Gurdwara Sahib where they perform daily *Prakash*. Two Gurdwaras and a Shiv Mandir are the only places of worship still under the control of the community.

Thaan Sahib and all the other Mandirs in Kandahar are now occupied by local Muslims. A couple of Mandirs in Kandahar district are under the control of Hindus. As the local Hindu population left, these Mandirs became a free and lucrative property for mischievous elements. However, in villages, the people are simple, closer knit and property or land has lesser value and allurement. Hence, they are less likely to be illegally occupied. In West Punjab in Pakistan, abandoned Mandirs and Gurdwaras which are far away from district headquarters and cities lie unmolested. In some cases, the villagers (who are all Muslims) clean them at regular intervals which have prolonged the life of the abandoned buildings.

Other Mandirs

In addition to Kabul, there are Dargah Peer Rattan Nath Mandirs across Afghanistan including Ghazni, Jalalabad, Gardez and Kunduz among other places. There was also mention of a Ganesh Mandir in Gardez, Paktia province. However, no further information could be obtained about these Mandirs.

The Afghan Hindu diaspora has built Asamai Mandirs in Faridabad (near Delhi), London, Germany, Netherland and the USA. The largest community is in Germany where they have built six Mandirs, two in Cologne and one each in Frankfurt, Kassel, Essen and Hamburg.

The vast majority of Mandirs and Gurdwaras outside Kabul, Jalalabad and Ghazni, if not all, are now under illegal occupation of the miscreants from the majority community. The thousand odd Afghan Sikh and Hindu population has now dwindled and concentrated in Kabul, Jalalabad and Ghazni only.

References

1. Ram Saran Basin from Kabul informed the author on 10th August 2018.
2. Sadhu Singh Saathi. (1994). *Ithas Khalsa Diwan Afghanistan*. Jalalabad: Parchar Committee Khalsa Diwan Afghanistan.

3. R. Lee. (2002). *Adits, Caves, Karizi-Qanats, and Tunnels in Afghanistan: An Annotated Bibliography*. Revised in November 2005.
4. https://www.hinduismtoday.com/modules/smartsection/item.php?itemid=3259. Accessed on 9th August 2018.
5. Ram Saran Basin from Kabul updated the author on 10th August 2018.
6. Information provided by a Hindu gentleman in Kandahar who spoke to the author during last week of May 2018 and February 2019. This gentleman also referred to the Chehel Dokhtaran which led the author to research more on it. Ganda Singh has mentioned it in his book.

15

Turbulent Years, Exodus and the Taliban

Mohammed Daud Khan, who was the first cousin of the ruler, Zahir Shah deposed him in 1973 in a bloodless coup. He declared Afghanistan a Republic state and became its first President. He remained at the helm of affairs until he was assassinated in April 1978 by the members of the People Democratic Party of Afghanistan, the communist party. Within a year there were several uprisings against the government and the next President too was killed by a powerful party leader in October 1979 which led to the 'Soviet Intervention' in December 1979.

This Soviet Intervention lasted for a decade and Afghanistan became a battleground for the Cold War. The USA and its allies started providing weapons to the Mujahideen to fight a 'proxy war' against the Soviet occupation. The Soviet withdrew in 1989 and handed over the defence to Afghan forces who were no match to the Mujahideen. The Mujahideen captured Kabul in 1992 and deposed President Najibullah.

The above civil war affected the people of Afghanistan. The rich Afghans including Muslims, Hindus and Sikhs started leaving the country in the mid-eighties.

The Afghan Sikh community was directly targeted in 1988 which shocked the community.

In 1988, on the first day of the *Vaisakhi Samagham*[1] at Jalalabad, the *Sangat* were going to *Langar* (community kitchen) when suddenly a man with an AK-47 rifle entered the Gurdwara complex and started firing at the devotees. Then as he tried to enter the Gurdwara Hall, Daler Singh, a Sikh soldier stood in front of him and shot all his bullets killing the assailant. However, in the process, Singh received several bullet injuries and died as well. In total, thirteen Sikhs and four Afghan Muslim soldiers were killed.

The next day was Election Day for the Parliament in Afghanistan. In Jalalabad, Bhai Darbari Singh was contesting the election. In Kabul, Gajinder Singh Rangila and Lala Tek Chand Sarin were in the fray. However, the above incident left a deep impact on the minds of the Hindus and Sikhs of Afghanistan and many did not come out to vote. Only Gajinder Singh Rangila was able to win his seat.

It was also the first time that Afghan TV broadcast *Gurbani* for half an hour where Bhai Amarjeet Singh Taan sang *Awal Allah Noor Upaya* and *Khalsa Mero Roop Hai Khas*. During *Vaisakhi*, Radio Kabul and Nangarhar would broadcast a special programme where people were informed about the Sikh religion and Guru Nanak[2].

Eminent Indian journalist Shekhar Gupta went to Kabul in May 1988, a month after the Sikh killings in Jalalabad and wrote his observations of Kabul currency market for the *India Today* magazine. The city's money market was described as Kabul's stock exchange, national reserve bank and social hubbub all rolled into one. In this unique market he saw currency notes piled high on shop counters and people walking in, accompanied by labourers carrying gunny bags full of cash on their backs! The officials estimated that seven to eight million dollars exchanged hands in the market every day. The majority of the thousand odd businessmen and jobbers were Afghan Sikhs and Hindus. Gupta notes that their acumen and honesty has made these people the richest community of Afghanistan. It seemed that the killings in Jalalabad a month ago had failed to deter the resilient community[3].

In 1989 the Mujahideen surrounded Jalalabad and started attacking it with rockets and this continued for nine months. People lost lives and left the city to escape the bombardment. During this time a rocket fell on the Gurdwara Guru Tegh Bahadur Sahib where a congregation had gathered. Seventeen Sikhs were killed and the Gurdwara was damaged. Following this incident, a lot of Sikhs and Hindus left the city and went to Kabul and Peshawar.

However, eleven months hence in April 1989, the *India Today* reported that the 50,000 odd Sikhs and Hindus who dominate the foreign trade and the money exchange business, were living in fear in Afghanistan.

The war with the Mujahideen in Jalalabad had led the Afghan Sikhs and Hindus to leave the city. Most of the community in Kandahar, Khost and Jalalabad were now in Kabul. The community was unhappy that the Indian Embassy in Kabul was 'much too stingy in issuing visas' allegedly at the behest of Afghan government as any large-scale departure of the community from Afghanistan would burst the official bubble that there was no panic in Kabul. The Indian Embassy had not replaced the six top diplomats, including the ambassador, who had left in the recent past. The Embassy was operating on a skeletal staff led by four diplomats[4].

In 1992, the Mujahideen won the last bastion, the capital Kabul. A large number of Afghan Sikhs and Hindus of Afghanistan started the exodus and left the country for good. Within a few months, when Rabani took the helm of affairs in the country, the Mujahideen factions revolted and the country plunged into yet another civil war[5].

Gajinder Singh was the Member of Parliament in Afghanistan from 1988–92. He played a pivotal role in 1992, working with Dr Najibullah Ahmadzai, the President of Afghanistan to get a safe passage for the Afghan Sikhs and Hindus.

The relations between Afghanistan and India were always cordial. It was felt that under the fundamentalist Mujahideen (who were supported by Pakistan and USA) life would become very difficult for the Afghan Sikhs and Hindus. These fears proved right later on as within months Afghanistan plunged into civil war when the Mujahideen factions started fighting among themselves.

At that time it was extremely bureaucratic to obtain a passport for anyone in Afghanistan. Nevertheless, the

Afghan government issued speedier passports to the Afghan Hindus and Sikhs and called the scheme *Aab Gang* (*Aab* means water, *Gang* is river Ganga) pilgrimage passport. It was on the lines of the Haj visa for Muslims issued by Saudi Arabia.

The Indian embassy set up an on-the-go visa department at Gurdwara Guru Har Rai Sahib in Shor Bazaar in Kabul to rapidly issue visas without any checks so that the Afghan Hindus and Sikhs could flee the civil war. It was too dangerous for people living in the old town to travel to the Indian embassy in the centre of the town because of the dangers of bombardment all over Kabul. The Indian embassy did not have enough staff to put the visa stamps so some Afghan Sikh volunteers at the Gurdwara had to put visa stamps on people's passports. Close to 50,000 people left Afghanistan and came to India under this scheme[6].

The above major exodus of the Afghan Sikhs and Hindus in 1992 happened just before the Mujahideen captured the capital Kabul[5]. Within a year, the Mujahideen factions started fighting among themselves and the country plunged into yet another civil war.

Life under the Taliban

By 1996, the Taliban, a Sunni Islamic fundamentalist group had captured most of Afghanistan and when they captured Kabul in September that year, 90 percent of the country was under them except for the parts of Northern Afghanistan. There is a remarkable anecdote of courage and determination displayed by the Afghan Sikhs during this period in Jalalabad[7].

The original Taliban were from the Kandahar region of Afghanistan. However, they were people from Pakistan and Saudi Arabia within their ranks as well. These Taliban (not the Afghan ones) would spit on the road at the sight of the Sikhs. The Sikhs wore a distinct style of turban and most of them would tie their beard, unlike the natives. The untrimmed moustaches of Sikh men were another distinction. The Sikhs were disgusted at this behaviour but tolerated it as they were the minuscule minority and the Taliban had guns with them.

One fine day in late 1996/97 at Tanda Bazaar in Jalalabad, the Sikhs were running their shops (cloth, grocery, Greco-Arabic medicine clinics) when a group of Taliban guards entered the bazaar and as usual one of them spit at a Sikh who was standing outside his cloth shop. Rather than spitting on the ground which was the norm, this Taliban spat on the face of the Sikh shopkeeper. This infuriated the Sikh as this act had crossed all limits of decency. He pulled his metre rod (used to measure cloth) which is made of steel and hit the Taliban on his head. The guard was not expecting such a reaction and after recovering from the shock he and the other guards pulled up their automatic rifles at the Sikh shopkeeper. By this time, the other Sikh traders from nearby shops gathered at the site and they scuffled with the Taliban guards and grabbed their rifles. The Taliban ran away and the Sikhs started shouting the Sikh slogan (known as *Jaikara*) *'Jo Bole So Nihal Sat Shri Akaal'*[8].

The matter was reported to the local Taliban chief who was an Afghan. He was aware of the Sikh religion and listened to both sides of the story. The Sikhs told him that they just wanted to run their shops but could not tolerate the humiliations meted out by the Talibanis. They added that though the rifles are the property of the Taliban, they were snatched in self-defence by the Sikhs during the scuffle. The chief disapproved of the spitting and it was decided that the Taliban initiated the fight and the Sikhs defended themselves. The Taliban guard who had spat expressed his ignorance about the Sikh religion.

Although it was not said in so many words, the Hanafi School of Islam allowed non-Muslims to live as *Dhimmis* (protected status) subject to the payment of *Jizya*. The Taliban chief asked how his men could differentiate the Sikhs from others. The chief was told about the Sikh religion and the turban but he was only interested to find a way for his men to differentiate between local Muslims and non-Muslims (Sikhs and Hindus). The Afghan Sikhs were told that they need to have a *Khanda* (symbol of Sikh faith) outside their houses. There were about fifty to sixty Afghan Sikh-Hindu families in Jalalabad and they felt that this would lead to 'target attacks'. This was not taken forward. The Afghan Hindus were asked to wear caps and yellow *tilak* (mark on the forehead) While the Afghan Hindu and Sikh women were asked to put a *bindi* (coloured dot in the centre of the forehead) and wear a *chador* (a cloak which covered the upper part of the body).

The Afghan Sikhs were not asked to wear a *tilak*, however they were often asked to convert. The logic was given that they were monotheistic, do not indulge in idol worship and have beards and wore turbans like Muslims. In such situations, the Afghan Sikhs would explain about their faith and tell the Taliban that they were happy and as God is one, all would go to Him after death. When asked why they kept on asking them to convert, the usual answer would be that their Prophet had told them to bring people to the 'true faith'.

All shopkeepers including Afghan Sikhs and Hindus were strictly told that they should not serve any woman who was not accompanied by an adult male from the family (husband, father or son only). If a woman was seen on the road alone then the Taliban would whip her. The Taliban and their strict and fundamentalist interpretation of Islam meant that local Muslims too were sometimes flogged in public but after this incident, the Taliban guards stopped spitting and largely left the Sikhs and Hindus alone. This identification was also implemented in Kabul and the rest of the country. The Afghan Sikhs and Hindus paid *Jizya* and were mostly left alone by the Taliban.

The Taliban continued to rule Afghanistan till October 2001. The American Air Force provided strategic support to the Northern Alliance on the ground in October 2001 and they managed to defeat the Taliban in a couple of months.

When the Taliban came to power in 1996 they banned televisions and transmission was stopped. Televisions were publically smashed and declared un-Islamic. Radio transmission was allowed but for religious programmes and Koranic verses only.

Five years later when the Taliban was defeated in October 2001, television transmission was resumed. The first broadcast after over five years was music and the news was co-presented by two Afghan women. It was a symbolic gesture as women and music were both shunned out of public life in the country under the Taliban. The first lines of the broadcast were, 'Greetings, viewers, we hope you are all well! We're glad to have destroyed terrorism and the Taliban and to be able to present this programme to you'[9].

With international support, Afghanistan started rebuilding its infrastructure and within a few years a number of private channels began airing.

Democratic government

Hamid Karzai was elected as the Interim Head of the Administration in December 2001 and later the President in 2002 by the grand assembly (*Loya Jirga*). He won the first Presidential election in 2004 and the second one in 2009. His second term ended in September 2014.

The initial few years of the Karzai administration was peaceful and there was a lot of hope and goodwill among people. About twenty-five Afghan Sikh and Hindu men and five families came back to Afghanistan from India. An Afghan Sikh informs that in 2002/03 he tried selling his house to the illegal occupier who offered him a price which was two-third of the prevailing market price. Ten years later he was still offered only half of the price quoted in 2002/03. A number of ex-warlords had joined the government and the goodwill had evaporated by then. The chance of the government enacting a law to restore the properties of the Afghan Sikhs and Hindus is very remote, hence, the illegal occupiers do not feel the need to pay anything but peanuts.

Pritpal Singh of the *Mission Afghanistan* documentary fame informed that his Greco-Arabic physician father's clinic (known as *Unani Dawakhana*) in Jade Maiwand Bazaar of Kabul is illegally occupied. Another Afghan Sikh told that his orchards and agricultural land outside Kabul city has been occupied by the caretakers themselves and they all belong to the majority community. Almost all the Afghan Sikhs and Hindus now live in Gurdwaras in Afghanistan in the absence of houses.

The Afghan Sikhs who left the country in 2015 and 2016, opine that life under the Taliban regime was 'not that bad'. The Afghan Sikhs and Hindus paid *Jizya* and were not bothered. However, under the present government, the locals keep on pestering them about conversion to the 'true faith' and their children get bullied in schools too. In every walk of life, they are discriminated against. Law and order has now (2018) deteriorated and cities frequently face suicide attacks and bomb blasts.

At present, there are about 850 Sikhs and sixty odd Hindus in Afghanistan and the majority of them live in and around Kabul, Ghazni and Jalalabad. The majority of Hindus are in Kabul and are from the Khost province[10].

References

1. A major festival in Sikh religion, in 1699 Guru Gobind Singh, the tenth and last Guru of the Sikhs administered *Khande di Pahul* (similar to baptism) and made *Nanakpanthi* community into Khalsa. *Vaisakhi* is celebrated on 13th April.
2. Khajinder S. Khurana. (2001). *Kabul de Sangat tee Afghanistan da Sankhep Ithas*. New Delhi.
3. https://www.indiatoday.in/magazine/international/story/19880531-men-of-indian-origin-dominate-currency-trade-in-afghanistan-797277-1988-05-31. Accessed on 3 February 2019.
4. https://www.indiatoday.in/magazine/special-report/story/19890415-hindu-and-sikh-community-in-afghanistan-live-under-constant-fear-today-815961-1989-04-15. Accessed on 3 February 2019.
5. Khajinder S. Khurana. (2001). *Kabul de Sangat tee Afghanistan da Sankhep Ithas*. New Delhi.
6. Pritpal Singh spoke to the son of Gajinder Singh and confirmed this information. All three are based in London.
7. Afghan Sikhs who now live in the UK related this incident to the author. They also informed that the very rich Afghan Hindus and Sikhs left the country in the 1980s, from 1983 onwards.
8. '*Jo Bole So Nihal Sat Sri Akal*' is the Sikh slogan or *Jaikara* (it is a shout of victory, triumph or exultation) which means one will be blessed eternally who says that God is the ultimate truth. It is an integral part of the Sikh religious service and is shouted at the end of *Ardas*, Sikh prayers and said in *Sangat* or holy congregation.

This is also the war cry of the Sikh regiment (and the Sikh Light Infantry) in the Indian Army.

9. http://news.bbc.co.uk/1/hi/world/south_asia/1663414.stm. Accessed on 20 August 2018.

10. Ram Saran Basin from Kabul updated the author during the first week of August 2018. The majority of the Khost community is Pashto-speaking *Sahajdhari* Sikhs.

16

Present Status and the Future

Khurana puts the number of Afghan Sikhs and Hindus in 1992 at around 60,000 and notes that 99 percent of them have left Afghanistan[1]. This seems like a more realistic figure although numbers as high as 220,000 have also been mentioned for Afghan Sikhs and Hindus.

Louis Dupree in his famous work, *Afghanistan* published in 1973 gives a humble figure of 25,000 for Afghan Sikhs and Hindus. He states that the majority of them were Sikhs who numbered about 15,000 and the rest were Hindus[2]. According to the prominent Sikhs in Kabul the number of Gurdwaras in Afghanistan exceeds sixty[3]. There were more than fifteen Hindu temples in Kandahar alone.

The Sikhs and Hindus were once an important part of the Afghan society, however, only a thousand of them now live in the country and the vast majority of them are Sikhs. Almost all of them live in Kabul, Jalalabad and Ghazni. In other places, Sikhs and Hindus have left long ago due to the deteriorating law and order situation. In Kandahar, there are a handful of Hindus, numbering less than ten. In Helmand, there are one or two Sikhs only. In some cases, they are shopkeepers and live alone as they have sent their families to India or abroad for safety concerns.

Mission Afghanistan documentary

The groundbreaking documentary *Mission Afghanistan* by Pritpal Singh shot during his visit to the country in October 2012 was released on the London-based Sikh TV channel, Sangat TV, in early 2013. The Guru Nanak Darbar—the Gurdwara Sahib run by the Afghan Sikhs in Southall, London partly funded the trip. The documentary was also featured in the *Sikh International Film Festival* of Toronto and aired on many TV channels around the world. Later, it was uploaded on *YouTube* and has since been viewed close to a million times.

Pritpal sent the copies of the documentary to the Home Offices of fourteen different EU countries. The receipt was duly acknowledged. This raised the awareness about the status of the Afghan Sikhs and Hindus. One of the achievements of this documentary was that the deportation of the Afghan Sikhs and Hindus stopped. Only one person has since been deported which happened last year.

After the documentary, the Afghan Sikh congregation at Guru Nanak Darbar sent £17,000 over to Afghanistan for their fellow brothers and sisters. The Afghan Sikhs in Dubai renovated the Khalsa Gurdwara in Kabul and the Afghan Sikhs settled in Europe paid to complete the pending construction of Gurdwara Guru Har Rai Sahib also in Kabul. The Afghan Sikh community in

Europe also renovated a Gurdwara in the new town of Charikar in Parwan province.

A vast majority of Afghan Sikhs and Hindus have lost their homes during the Afghan civil war. Many have property papers but are forced to live in Gurdwaras as their houses have been illegally occupied by the miscreants from the majority community.

Status of Gurdwaras and temples

In 1992, when the Afghan Sikhs and Hindus started to leave the country they left their places of worship which also played the role of community centres under some Sikh and Hindu caretakers. The law and order situation did not improve and after some years even the caretakers left. And finding the Gurdwaras and temples empty, some miscreants and opportunists from the majority community occupied them. In some cases, 'reliable' Muslim caretakers were nominated but after some time these caretakers too refused to vacate the building. The vast majority of Afghan Sikh and Hindu places of worship outside Kabul, Jalalabad and Ghazni are now illegally occupied by the local Muslim population[4].

Interestingly, none of the Afghan Sikhs and Hindus inside and outside Afghanistan volunteered this information. However, when asked to confirm they did not deny it either. There is an obvious fear of backlash for the small community still remaining in Afghanistan. Kandahar, a prominent city in southern Afghanistan was once home to substantial numbers of Hindus and Sikhs. Seventy percent of them were Hindus and the city had eighteen to twenty temples along with five Gurdwaras known by their old name, *Dharamsaal*. The latter has been covered in some detail by Prof. Ganda Singh.

With one exception, all temples are now under the illegal occupation of unscrupulous elements from the majority community. Some of these occupiers claim that the temples had been sold to them but are unable to provide receipts. Ischer Dass has written that the Mandirs and Gurdwaras are registered in the name of individuals and families in Afghanistan (unlike mosques). It is alleged that two Gurdwaras in Kandahar have been sold by a couple of Afghan Sikhs themselves. The new local Muslim 'owners' have built additional storeys over the existing buildings. A person conversant with the Sikh values and behaviour would know a Gurdwara is considered the property of the *Sangat* (Sikh congregation) and only a local congregation can unanimously take such important decisions.

There are five Hindus and four Sikhs now living in one *Dharamsaal*. The *Dharamsaal* of Baba Sri Chand is still under the possession of the Sikh community however, it is empty. A seventy-four-year-old bachelor Hindu physician at Kandahar still runs his clinic and has dedicated his life to the community. This physician visits his nephew in India every year for a few weeks but returns to Kandahar every time. He along with a few Sikhs in Kabul are one of the few educated and reasonably well-off people who could leave

Afghanistan easily but have committed their lives to the community[5].

In the neighbouring Helmand province, the capital Lashkargah had two Gurdwaras but the entire Hindu and Sikh population except for two Sikhs have left the province and the country for good. These Sikhs are the shopkeepers who are running their shops and looking after the Gurdwaras. Their families in agreement have migrated to India or other countries for safety. This was according to the last information received from Helmand. On 29th December 2016, an Afghan Sikh Nirmohan Singh, fondly known as Lala Dilsoz, was killed by armed gunmen in Kunduz which led to the exodus of the remaining Afghan Sikhs and Hindus from the province. There is a handful of the community in other cities now.

The cremation grounds in several cities have been illegally occupied. In Kabul, the Afghan Sikhs and Hindus have to ring the police to send security so that they could cremate their dead without the local Muslim throwing stones at them. This is also the case in Jalalabad and Ghazni.

Terror revisits Jalalabad

On 1st July 2018, in a suicide bombing at Jalalabad, fifteen Afghan Sikhs and four Afghan Hindus were killed. They had been travelling in a vehicle to meet President Ashraf Ghani, who was visiting Nangarhar province when the bomber struck. Among those killed was the one Sikh candidate who had planned to contest October's parliamentary elections, Avatar Singh

Khalsa[6] and his close associate Rawail Singh. Both of them had served in the Afghan National Army and provided leadership to the Afghan Sikhs and Hindu community. They could have left the country long ago but continued to stay to look after the interests of the remaining members of the community. Many important Afghan Sikhs and Hindus were killed as well that took away almost the entire leadership of the community. Subsequently, few families went to India to seek refugee status.

This cowardly act was widely condemned within and outside Afghanistan. A protest march was taken out in Kabul by locals in support of the Afghan Sikhs and Hindus. Similar peaceful protests were arranged across the globe. Dr Shaida Abdali, the Afghan Ambassador to India tweeted: 'I'm really short of words to express our shock and sadness on the loss of our most patriotic Afghans in Jalalabad—the least I can say: it was indeed an attack on Afghan patriotism, religious freedom, diversity, democracy, Indo-Afghan friendship and shared values.'

Three days after this suicide attack, some miscreants came outside the Bhai Mansa Singh Gurdwara in Kabul at night and tried to force their way into the premises. They shouted and kicked the gate a number of times. Unable to break the gate, they shouted *'kafirs'* and fired a few times in the air. Land in Kabul is expensive and the Gurdwaras in Kabul are relatively big and seen as lucrative property. Like other Gurdwaras in Kabul, it houses a number of Sikh families. Some miscreants probably thought that they can use suicide bombing as an opportunity to further terrify the residents and later grab the property. It was reported to the local police the next day.

Later that month (July 2018), the Khost community from Kabul came to their ancestral province to repair the Gurdwara which was hit by a rocket-missile in December 1992 in retaliation to the demolition of the disputed Babri Masjid in Ayodhya in India. Many Gurdwaras and Mandirs were attacked all across Afghanistan in December that year. This was also a symbolic gesture of defiance[7]. Dr Anarkali Honaryar, the former Sikh woman parliamentarian who is also from the Khost community and Narinder Pal Singh Khalsa are now perhaps the only known names left in the community.

On 1st September 2018 a Sikh was shot at in his shop in Herat, the third largest city of the country situated in western Afghanistan close to the Iranian border. The Guru Arjan Gurdwara in Delhi, managed by the Afghan Sikhs immediately arranged tickets and visa for the Sikh and his family. The Sikh was operated on in Delhi and the two bullets were removed. He is now healthy. This was yet another case of targeted/marked attack as the Sikhs due to their turban and unshaven facial hair are easily identifiable. Before the attack there were three Sikh families and eleven individuals in total. Following this attack, only two Sikhs remain in Herat. The rest have migrated to India. Prior to 1990 many of them used to live in Herat. An area called Serai Hinduian (Caravanserai of Hindus) and a cremation ground are the only remaining remnants of Afghan Sikhs and Hindus in the city now. The cremation ground has been illegally occupied and houses have been built by the majority community[8]. The Sikh and Hindu students are harassed and bullied in schools by Muslim pupils who call them *kafir* and tell them that they can't study with them. The teachers, it seems, do little to discourage them. In mundane life, the Sikhs and Hindus are often asked when they are going back to their country, India! Let's examine this allegation that Afghan Hindus and Sikhs are recent migrants from India.

The Afghan Sikhs and Hindus will tell that their great-grandfathers were born in the country. The average Afghan does not know their history well except the propaganda that nobody has ever defeated or ruled Afghanistan. For most Afghan Muslims, Islam came in the seventh century and with a big bang everyone converted to Islam. The Kandahar and Zabul province till mid-ninth century, Kabulistan till mid-10th century and Ghor province till 11th century were ruled by infidels, Buddhist and/or Hindus. The Ghaznavid rulers in the 11th century hired Hindus in their army to neutralise their opponents. Then in the 13th century, the country was devastated and ruled by infidel Mongols for three-fourths of a century. Later, they converted to Islam. Contemporary historians in the late 14th century have given accounts of how Timur's (who ruled most of present Afghanistan) capital Samarkand was attacked numerous times by 'idol worshippers'.

Babur who started the Mughal dynasty came from present-day Uzbekistan and captured Kabul in 1504 and later North India in 1526. Even when Babur had not captured Delhi, had noted that Kabul was an important trading centre for merchants from Hindustan. Guru Nanak, the founder of the Sikh religion, visited Afghanistan during this period and gave hope to the minorities living in the country. The Sikh preachers were nominated in Kabul and there are numerous instances where the Sikhs from Kabul and Peshawar came to Punjab to pay their respects to the Sikh Gurus (1469–1708). For the next 200 years until 1738, Mughals based in Delhi and Agra ruled most of North-Eastern Afghanistan and at times Kandahar as well. People moved within provinces and Kabulistan was a part of Hindustan.

Then Ahmed Shah 'Baba', during his reign appointed infidel Hindus as governors of Kashmir and Punjab. During his eight looting expeditions to North India, he brought the Mughal Empire to its knees and made them penniless. The numerous British accounts from the late 18th and 19th century give references of Hindu and Sikh traders in Afghanistan. All this time until Amir Abdur Rahman in 1896 attacked and brought them under Islam, the province of Kafirstan continued to be 'pagan' and indulge in idol worship. Once the Amir converted them to Islam he renamed the province Nuristan. For those who think that Hindus and Sikhs in Afghanistan are not Afghan, they need a lesson in history.

The Afghan Sikhs and Hindus are frequently told that they should convert as it is not possible to be an Afghan and a non-Muslim! Alas, gone are the days of Amirs Amanullah and Zahir Shah who worked for a diverse and pluralistic Afghanistan[9].

The Afghan Sikhs and Hindus have received support from unexpected quarters on their ancestry. On 15th July 2018, a memorial service was held at the Afghanistan Embassy in Washington DC for the nineteen Afghan Sikhs and Hindus who were killed in a terrorist attack in Jalalabad on 1st July 2018.

Hamdullah Mohi, the Afghan Ambassador to the USA said at the memorial service, 'This occasion is one that brings us together to recognise a community that has deep roots in Afghanistan. For many, they often think of the minority Hindus and Sikhs as migrants from India. But in reality, the Hindus and Sikhs of Afghanistan are the original residents of this country'.

The Ambassador-at-Large for International Religious Freedom Sam Brownback added, 'The Sikh and Hindu communities have a long and distinguished heritage and this horrific attack will not diminish that. Our office will continue to monitor the conditions faced by religious minorities in Afghanistan. I stand with you and will work toward an Afghanistan that is peaceful and secure for all its people'[10].

Sadly, the Afghan government has done little regarding the forcible occupation of the houses of Afghan Sikhs and Hindus and their places of worship. Not a single Afghan Sikh or Hindu is currently enrolled in higher education and even in high school. This has been the case for the past twenty years and none of the Afghan Sikhs and Hindus in their 20s, 30s and even early 40s are educated beyond high school. In the previous generation, we had doctors, professors, engineers and other professionals. The Afghan Sikhs and Hindus are not allowed to work within the administration and none are employed in the public sector. They are discriminated against at every sphere of public life. They are told to convert and threatened with abduction and conversion of their daughters[11]. Will the conversion of the minorities (who number just around 900) solve the Afghan problem? Almost 99.99 percent of the population is Muslim then why is Afghanistan still such a bitterly divided nation?

In 2017, on the Sikh festival of *Vaisakhi*, the foundation stone of the first-ever school for Sikh and Hindu students was laid in Jalalabad, Nangarhar province. It was funded by the Swedish International Development Cooperation Agency (SIDA). Pajhwok News Agency reported that the school with six classrooms, a library, separate offices, five toilets and desks and chairs would be completed within six months at a cost of 8.9 million Afghanis.

Pajhwok added that the sixty Sikh-Hindu students who are studying in the temporary school established in the temple will be transferred to this modern primary school on completion. A similar school has been constructed in Ghazni for Sikh-Hindu students[12].

However, these are primary schools and the problem of bullying by Muslim students continues in Kabul and high schools. The teachers silently witness this bullying thereby encouraging the bullies. Sadly, the teachers have forgotten the contribution of the Afghan Sikhs and Hindus including the role of Diwan Niranjan Das, an Afghan Hindu, in negotiating the freedom of Afghanistan with the British in 1921[13].

Speaking to Al-Jazeera TV channel on 1st January 2017, Rawail Singh summed up the miseries of the community, 'There is only so much a community can tolerate. We can't practise our faith openly; our children can't go to school because of harassment; we can't even cremate our dead without being stoned by the public'. Al-Jazeera added that he was referring to the 2012 incident when civilians and security forces prevented them from performing funeral rites at their ancient cremation grounds, parts of which had been taken over by armed locals[14].

Discrimination against Afghan Sikhs and Hindus is well documented. USA's Bureau of Democracy, Human Rights and Labor department's 2017 report on Afghanistan states, 'Afghan Sikhs and Hindus faced discrimination, including unequal access to government jobs and harassment in school, as well as verbal and physical abuse in public places'[15].

The entire generation of Afghan Sikhs and Hindus, after 1992 have not been able to study initially due to civil war and then due to unending bullying by fellow students from the majority community. The Afghan Sikhs (and Hindus) in their 20s and 30s whose families did not leave Afghanistan until a few years ago have not completed their schooling. Most of them have studied in the Gurdwaras and are conversant with the Gurmukhi script but have not completed their school leaving qualification. They can speak the local Afghan languages, Dari and Pashto but cannot read or write them[16].

The generation before 1992 was qualified and one could find doctors, lawyers, teacher, lecturers, accountants and other professionals among them. The following generation who are settled abroad informed that although they had studied in schools which were run by Afghan Sikhs and Hindus, post 1992, these schools were also closed as teachers and other staff had left the country. The lack of education among their children is a huge concern for the Afghan Sikhs (and Hindus) still living in the country.

Due to discrimination, young girls are not allowed to go outside. Parents are worried about their daughters and the prospect of finding a suitable match is very slim. Education among the Afghan Sikh and Hindu women is even worse than men. An Afghan Sikh reported that his wife was denied blood transfusion in the government hospital despite the availability of blood in the blood bank. The hospital argued that the available Muslim blood cannot be given to a non-Muslim. It was only when the Afghan Sikh raised the issue with higher authorities in local government that transfusion was done.

Vote-bank politics

The Indian government has provided refuge to the Afghan Hindu-Sikh and Sindhi Hindu refugees but few have managed to get the citizenship. The first Afghan Hindu-Sikh refugee came to India in 1979 and many followed in subsequent years. Forty years hence, only one-third of the Afghan Hindus and Sikhs have been given Indian citizenship. Some Sindhi Hindus had gone back and a few Afghan Sikhs and Hindus also returned to Afghanistan when Hamid Karzai came to power after the fall of the Taliban in 2001. However, after a few years, the 'feel good' factor evaporated and 'the warlords' joined the government. The properties of Afghan Sikhs and Hindus are under illegal occupation of the former caretakers, neighbours and sometimes the 'powerful' elite. The Afghan government does not seem to have any plan to secure the properties of at least those Afghan Sikhs and Hindus who are still in the country.

Democracy in third world countries is dictated by vote-bank politics. Afghan Sikhs and Hindus do not form a vote-bank because of their small numbers hence, neither India nor Afghanistan, supposed to be friendly nations, discuss this issue. A few years ago when the Indian prime minister came to Kabul he could not find time to meet the Afghan Sikh-Hindu community. There are a number of Afghan Muslims living and working in New Delhi as refugees without being discriminated against. While in Afghanistan, the original inhabitants of the land, the Afghan Hindus and Sikhs are reminded every day that they are *kafirs* and not native of Afghanistan. They are asked when they would be leaving and going back to India while in India, they are referred to as Afghans!

It is high time that the Afghan government created a department to look after Evacuee Properties. The Evacuee Properties Trust Board (EPTB) looks after the Sikh Gurdwaras and Hindu temples left behind following the partition in Pakistan. Although some corrupt officials have sold some abandoned places of worship and built shopping malls, it has also re-opened a number of Gurdwaras and Mandirs after political pressure and court orders. The Afghan Sikhs and Hindus are afraid of backlash, hence they shy away from publicly raising the issue of illegal occupation of their houses, schools and businesses.

Silver lining

The suicide bombing in Jalalabad in July 2018 finally woke up India and the rest of the world about the dangers that the Afghan Hindus and Sikhs face every day. In India, the Citizenship (Amendment) Bill, 2016 which was passed by the Lok Sabha in January 2019 amended the Citizenship Act, 1955 to make Hindus, Sikhs, Buddhists, Jains, Parsis and Christians from three Muslim-majority countries—Bangladesh, Pakistan and Afghanistan—eligible for Indian citizenship. This means that the migrants belonging to these religious communities who entered India without the necessary documents prior to 2014 would not be imprisoned or deported and would gain permanent citizenship after six years of residency in India. This is a welcome piece of news and a big gift for the Afghan Hindus and Sikhs living in the country

In late November 2018, the Government of Canada approved the resettlement of Sikh and Hindu refugees to Canada, who had fled Afghanistan due to religious persecution. The applications of the Afghan Sikhs and Hindus were privately sponsored by the Manmeet Singh Bhullar Foundation and the World Sikh Organization of Canada.

Divided nation

The biggest problem Afghanistan faces is that it is a divided nation—divided along tribal lines. In his biography, Amir Abdur Rahman (1880–1901) described the political atmosphere of Afghanistan when he started his reign, 'Every priest, mullah, and chief of every tribe considered himself an independent King, and for about 200 years past, the freedom and independence of many of these priests were never broken by their sovereigns'[17].

More than a century later this problem still exists to some extent, precipitated by the long civil war. The Pashtun form 40–45 percent of the population and all rulers and Presidents have been from this community. They have failed to embrace the diversity and are not seen to be inclusive. In 2015, the Afghan government tried to implement the biometric ID cards for citizens but ethnicity became a big issue as everyone was identified as Afghan on the cards. The intended meaning was 'Afghanistan nationals', but for many, the term implied a reference to Pashtuns, hence, it failed to give proper recognition to other ethnicities like Tajiks, Uzbeks, Hazaras and others[18].

In this hierarchy, the Hazaras are at the bottom as they are Shia Muslims, unlike the others who are Sunnis. They are easily identified due to their partial Mongolian features and are discriminated against. Below them come the Afghan Sikhs and Hindus as they are not even Muslim and hence infidels. For most Afghans, it is impossible to comprehend that an Afghan can be anything but Muslim.

References

1. Khajinder S. Khurana. (2001). *Kabul de Sangat tee Afghanistan da Sankhep Ithas.* New Delhi.
2. Louis Dupree. (1973). *Afghanistan.* New York: Princeton University Press. In another part of the book he puts the number of Afghan Sikhs and Hindus at 30,000.
3. Sadhu Singh Saathi. (1994). *Ithas Khalsa Diwan Afghanistan.* Jalalabad: Parchar Committee Khalsa Diwan Afghanistan.
4. Confirmed by multiple sources across Afghanistan.
5. Informed during a telephone conversation in the last week of May.
6. It was reported in Tolo news that Avtar Singh Khalsa lost ten members of his family in the Afghan conflict. Two of his brothers, who were army soldiers, were killed during the last three decades of fighting.
7. Pritpal Singh uploaded the video on his Facebook Page.
8. The author spoke to Satnam Singh on 28 September 2018. He informed that he came to Herat from Ghazni about eleven years ago. His grandfather was from Gardez. They couldn't find any Gurdwaras or Mandirs in Herat (probably occupied?). In Herat, Satnam Singh had a dedicated prayer room in his house where the families would gather and pray.
9. Covered across different chapters in this book.
10. https://www.news18.com/news/world/sikhs-hindus-original-residents-of-afghanistan-not-indian-migrants-afghan-envoy-1815019.html. Accessed on 15th August 2018.

11. An Afghan Sikh who left the country in 2015 informed the author that he was specifically told by a local that they will be targeting girls from the minority community to convert and marry them with local Muslims.
12. https://www.pajhwok.com/en/2017/04/13/work-school-building-sikhs-launched. Accessed on 8th July 2018.
13. Louis Dupree. (1973). *Afghanistan.* New York: Princeton University Press.
14. https://www.aljazeera.com/indepth/features/2016/12/decline-afghanistan-hindu-sikh-communities-161225082540860.html. Accessed on 8th July 2018.
15. Bureau of Democracy, Human Rights and Labor, Country Reports on Human Rights Practices for 2017. https://www.tolonews.com/afghanistan/us-report-highlights-violence-ethnic-tensions-afghanistan. Accessed on 8th July 2018.
16. Manmohan Singh living in Nottingham, UK informed the author that he was very concerned about the education of his children as they could not study in the local school due to bullying and harassment. They were told to convert. He left Afghanistan and came to the UK in November 2015.
17. Mir Sultan Mahomed Khan. (1900). *The Life of Abdur Rahman: Amir of Afghanistan.* London: John Murray.
18. https://iwpr.net/global-voices/ethnic-component-afghan-id-cards-still. Accessed on 10th August 2018.

17

Kafiristan, the Pagan Province of Afghanistan

The present province of Nuristan was known as Kafiristan (land of infidels) until 1895–96 when Amir Abdur Rahman occupied it and converted the occupants to Islam. The province borders Pakistan's Chitral district to the east which is home to pagan Kalash people who were co-religionist with the *kafirs*. The people of Kafiristan were fiercely independent with a distinctive culture, language and religion. Their religion was somewhat similar to ancient Hinduism. After the conquest, the Amir named the province Nuristan (land of illumination).

Alexander Gardner, a traveller of mixed-race ancestors by his own account, was in Afghanistan[1] between 1827–30 and visited Kafirstan. In 1831, he joined the artillery under Maharaja Ranjit Singh at Lahore and was later promoted to the rank of Colonel and remained in the Sikh army till 1846.

Gardner met and was hosted by an old *Peer* (holy man) who belonged to the clan of Nimchu *Kafirs*, who were the descendants of mixed unions between *Kafirs* and Muslims and were found 'all-round the borders of

Kafiristan'. The *Peer* told him that Scythia (land north of Black and Caspian Sea in Central Asia) was the original home of the *Kafir* race and claimed 'one of the kings of the dynasty of Cyrus as their founder'.

The *Peer* gave Gardner parting gifts which included a fine leopard-skin mantle with a matching cap, sixty gold *tillahs* (in a silk handkerchief) and a copy of the Koran. The *Peer* also provided a guide and along with him was a Hindu by the name of Jey Ram of 'respectable appearance and well-armed'. Gardner adds that they appeared to have travelled much together. They were both well-educated men, and could read, write, and speak fluently Persian, Turkish, Pashto and Arabic. Jey Ram also had 'some colloquial knowledge of the languages of Kafiristan' where he had travelled before with some other Hindus. Jey Ram had also been to many places in Russia including Moscow.

Gardner took a north-easterly direction through the Khojah Mahomed range and came to a pass called Kafir Ghesh Durrah. Here, he saw two large stone idols cut out of the solid rock. The idols were of *Kafir* deity Ghesh (the Earth) and his wife Dizane (the producer of all things).

Major Hugh Pearse who edited Gardner's memoirs writes that the full diary of this visit from Pamir to Kafiristan was lent to Alexander Burnes and was destroyed when the latter was murdered in 1841 at Kabul and his house was robbed.

Mohan Lal in his account[2] mentions a certain Mufti who had travelled to the country of *Siah Posh Kafirs* (black-robed infidels) and gave a brief account to Gerard (and Mohan Lal). It is a second-hand account but one of the earliest and less known ones. It is also fascinating how a Muslim (Mufti[3]) and a Hindu (Mohan Lal) interpret their customs.

The Mufti from Jalalabad went to Kanur, and then to Chaghul Sarae. He then passed through the valleys called Darrah Nur, Damanj, and Vakul. On the third day the Mufti arrived at the village named Katar, occupied by the *Siah Posh*.

The horse was not known to them and the inhabitants were surprised 'at some feats' performed by the Mufti's horse. The people were 'masters of beauty' and wore a dress made of goat's skin and let their hair hang down the shoulders. They drank wine and always sat on chairs.

They worshipped idols made of stone or wood and called them Baruk or Maha Dev. They wore iron rings in their ears and a string ornamented with shells round their necks. They sacrificed cows on their holidays and when asked where God is, they pointed their fingers towards the west (Mecca is towards the west). They read the 'Kalimah' to please Muslims but also confessed that they were *Kafirs*. They did not intermarry among their relations and their weddings were unusual and different. We are told, 'They bring their wives unveiled on their shoulders, dance, run, and jump in the streets (like a jackass, as the Mufti said), accompanied by crowds of men and women, who play upon drums and flutes, and make a great noise. The parents of the girl are exceedingly pleased to see the husband using his utmost exertions in jumping, as they think him in consequence the more devoted lover of his wife'.

They sent their pregnant women to a 'public receptacle' before their 'accouchement' and they were kept there for forty days. Men were not allowed to enter this place and only women served them.

The *Siah Posh* people did not mourn at funerals and in fact it was solemnised in a joyful manner. We are told that the corpse was attended by young men, 'who sing, skip, dance, and play upon drums, unwashed it is carried upon the shoulders of men, in a large box, to the top of a high mountain, and laid open in the sun. They sacrifice a cow and give a feast to the attendants of the funeral, and return home, not weeping at all'.

After sixty days, the body would have decayed or eaten by the birds. Then the women of the family in a group would go up the mountain and pick up the bones and wash them in a stream. The bones would be brought home and the women would sit around them and mourn for a short time. We are told 'After this the men come and convey the bones to a large cave, excavated in the ground. They throw them in it, and, turning to the bones, say, this is your heaven'.

The language of the *Siah Posh* was mixed with Hindustani, Persian and Afghani. They were good archers, used spears and carried swords around their waist and a shield on their backs. Mohan Lal writes, 'They fight with great ferocity, gnashing their teeth, and roaring like a lion. The victors are crowned with chaplets, made of the leaves of the mulberry-tree'.

The women managed all outdoor business and men looked after the kids and 'follow no employment, except that of occasional warfare'. The women produced fine rice, wheat and barley. The fruits were abundant and they made good wine from grapes. Instead of sugar, the *Siah Posh* used syrup of watermelons. They ate the meat of all animals except dogs and jackals. When a man committed adultery he was fined twelve or thirteen rupees and evoked no anger or jealousy among men. The men 'commend the liberality of their females towards every man, who is the best of God's creatures in the world'.

The *Siah Posh* people claimed descent from the Arabs but some of them stated that they descended from the Macedonian soldiers. The artists in Kafiristan were called *Bari*. They were treated badly by other *Siah Posh* and were not allowed to sit before them. They used force to sell the children of *Baris* to the Muslims of neighbouring provinces. The *Siah Posh* people called *Bari*, the descendants of those slaves 'which their lion-figured fathers brought at the invasion of India'. However, they do not mention particularly the name of Sikandar (Alexander).

Mohan Lal believes them to be the descendants of the Macedonian soldiers of Alexander but a number of recent DNA studies have stated that Nuristani and the Kalash people living in Chitral (same stock) have little or no Greek background[4].

Sir George Scott Robertson was a soldier and administrator, who is best known for his book *The Kafirs of the Hindu Kush*[5] which was based on his stay in

Kafiristan for over twelve months during 1890–91. The book provides a wealth of knowledge about the *Kafirs* and their culture, customs, traditions and religion. The book was published in 1896 which also coincided with the invasion of Kafiristan and subsequent conversion of the inhabitants to Islam by Amir Abdur Rahman Khan.

Robertson revealed that there was no literature or written character of any kind in Kafiristan. He writes that the dominant races of Kafiristan—the *Katirs*, the *Kdm*, and the *Wai*—have mainly descended from the ancient Indian population of Eastern Afghanistan that refused to embrace Islam in the 10th century and fled for refuge from the victorious Muslims to the hilly countries of Kafiristan. Robertson adds that there they found other races already settled, 'whom they vanquished, drove away, or enslaved, or with whom they amalgamated'. He adds that part of the slave population including the *Jazhis* and the *Aroms*, were remnants of these people. Robertson theorises that the *Fresuns* were probably a more or less aboriginal race, who either successfully resisted the new-comers 'or were driven from more fertile regions and milder altitudes to their present valley'.

Robertson makes a distinction between *Safeh Posh* (white-robed) and *Siah Posh* (black-robed) *Kafirs*. He writes that *Safeh Posh* tribes are entirely different from the *Siah Posh* tribes, 'They are remarkable for their more peaceful disposition, and their inefficiency as fighting men. They have patient stolid faces for the most part, and, compared with the *Kafirs*, are heavy in their movements. The thick clothes they wear add to their clumsy appearance. They are a simple people, very industrious, capable of wonderful feats of endurance, and, with the exception of the inhabitants of one of the villages, Pushkigrom, they are meek and poor-spirited'.

The religion of *Kafirs* is described as a low form of idolatry with an admixture of ancestor-worship and some traces of fire-worship also. There were a number of gods and goddesses with varying 'degree of importance or popularity'. Imra the Creator, Moni (commonly spoken of as 'the prophet') Gish the war-god, Bagisht, Dizane, Krumai, and Nirmali were common to all the tribes. There were several secondary deities peculiar to particular localities as well.

Robertson writes that the gods were worshipped by sacrifices, by dances, by singing hymns and by uttering invocations. Fairies and demons were appeased by sacrifices. He adds, 'The only phrase known to me which is comparable to our profane swearing is "*Shut Imrd di psdld*" (May the curse of God strike you)'.

We are told the principal gods and goddesses were Imra, Moni, Gish, Bagisht, Arom, Sanrn, Sataram (or Sudaram), Inthr, Dozhi, Nong, Parade, Shomde, Saranji (or Saaranjn), Dizane, Nirmali, Kramai (or Shamai).

Conquest of Kafiristan

The Amir of Afghanistan, Abdur Rahman Khan in his autobiography[6] has stated that the Russian conquest of the Pamirs made the region vulnerable, hence in the winter of 1895 the four columns of the imperial army surrounded and simultaneously attacked Kafiristan from all directions. The campaign was successful and within forty days the whole province of Kafiristan was conquered. Khan writes that when the Christian missionaries heard of his conquest, they made a great stir in England, stating that the *Kafirs* were their fellow Christians. Khan adds that he did not find any Christians among them and their religion 'was a curious mixture of ancient idol worships and superstitions'.

Those *Kafirs* that had fought bravely were taken prisoners and were settled in Paghman province near Kabul which has a climate similar to Kafiristan. The Amir writes that he opened several schools for their education. He calls them a very brave nation, and almost all of the young generation were trained for military service.

The impregnable fort of Kullum situated in the interior of Kafiristan was made a military station and the Afghans found an inscription at the gate which read, 'The Great Mogul Emperor Timour was the first Muslim conqueror who vanquished the country of this unruly people up to this point, but could not take Kullum, owing to its difficult position'.

The commanding officer, Captain Mahomed Ali Khan, engraved the following inscription upon the same stone, 'In the reign of Amir Abdur Rahman Ghazi, in 1896, the whole of Kafiristan, including Kullum, was conquered by him, and the inhabitants embraced the true and holy religion of Islam', and engraved a verse from the Koran, which means righteousness and virtue have come, and untruth has disappeared.

References

1. Maj. Hugh Pearse (Ed.). (1898). *Soldier and Traveller: Memoirs of Alexander Gardner*. London: William Blackwood.
2. Mohan Lal. (1846). *Travels in the Panjab, Afghanistan and Turkistan to Balk, Bokhara, and Herat and a Visit to Great Britain and Germany*. London: WH Allen & Co.
3. Mufti is an Islamic scholar who interprets Islamic laws and also acts as a jurist.
4. Sadaf Firasat, Shagufta Khaliq, *et al.* (2007). 'Y-chromosomal evidence for a limited Greek contribution to the Pathan population of Pakistan', *European Journal of Human Genetics*. Vol. 15, pp. 121–126.
5. Sultan Mahomed Khan (Ed.). (1900). *The Life of Abdur Rahman, Amir of Afghanistan*. London: John Murray.
6. George Scott Robertson. (1896). *The Kafirs of the Hindu Kush*. London: Lawrence & Bullen Ltd.

18

Hindus, Sahajdharis and Sikhs in Baluchistan

Baluchistan which shares a long border with Afghanistan has a significant Pashtun (known as Pathan in Pakistan) population and the Hindu and Sikh minority in the province share similarities with Afghan Hindus and Sikhs. Hence, it is imperative this topic is explored in some detail.

In 1810, Henry Pottinger refers to Hindus in Baluchistan, 'Hindus are to be found at the ports of Sonmiani and Gwadar, on the Las and Makran coast, but rarely, except at Kalat, in the towns of the interior'. He adds that they were the mercantile community of Multan and Shikarpur (Sindh).

Pottinger has stated the oral history tradition of Kalat, the interior city in Baluchistan which has the famous Goddess Kali temple said to belong to the pre-Islamic era. Pottinger has stated that Kalat was ruled by a Hindu dynasty for many centuries, and the last ruler was either named Sewah or that this was the hereditary title of the dynasty. In the seventh century, Islam came and Kambar formally deposed Sewah and forced numbers of Hindus to become Muslims. Sewah and a small portion of the population first went to Zehri where his son Sangin was ruling but the Muslim tribes overran Zehri and they eventually went to Shikarpur, Bakkar (Punjab) and Multan and 'obtained an asylum among the inhabitants there, who were principally of their own creed'. Later the rulers of Kalat reversed the policy of their ancestor Kambar and persuaded these Hindus to 'reside and trade within their territories'. How many years after Kambar was this policy reversed, is anyone's guess.

Pottinger adds that Mohbat Khan, a close confidante and contemporary of Nadir Shah, ruler of Persia who is notorious for his loot and destruction of North India in 1739, was a tyrant and held Hindus in 'such utter detestation that he did everything possible to prevent their remaining in his dominions'.

However, his brother Nasir Khan who was the successor encouraged Hindus to come back and trade and remitted many of the taxes imposed on merchandise by his brother. He fixed them on a moderate rate. Nasir Khan even revived the old grant made by one of his predecessors which allowed Hindus to impose a levy of 25 percent on every camel-load of goods entering the bazaar for the maintenance of the Goddess Kali temple and its priests at Kalat[1].

There were Hindus in important positions as well. Charles Masson (1844) refers to the Hindu agent, Diwan Bacha of the Khan of Kalat who looked after finances and represented the Khan in his dealing with the British[2].

Guru Nanak's visit to Baluchistan

In 1969, to coincide with the 500 years birth centenary celebration of Guru Nanak, Dr Kirpal produced a monumental work, *Janamsakhi Parampara* (Tradition) which contains a wealth of knowledge on the life and times of Guru Nanak. The work quotes *Miharban Janamsakhi* which contains a *Sakhi* titled *Guru Ji Hinglaj Vich* (Guru Ji at Hinglaj). The Hinglaj Devi temple is situated in Hingol National Park, Lasbela district of Baluchistan.. Guru Nanak visited this place on his journey to Mecca[3].

The temple is an important destination of Hindus living in Sindh and even receives devotees from India. The local Muslims call the shrine 'Nani Mandir' (temple of maternal grandmother). Charles Masson (1844) has given an interesting explanation that Hinglaj is also revered by the Muslims as the shrine of Bibi Nani (the Lady Nani). He further adds that it is possible people have preserved the ancient name Nanalaj, goddess of the ancient Persian and Bactrian people. Inanna was a Goddess in the ancient Sumerian civilisation and Nanna was a goddess in Notre culture. Nani in sub-continental languages means maternal grandmother.

When Guru Nanak reached the Valley of Hingol river, some sadhus came to meet him. They saw him attired like a Haji and were surprised at this. They could not make out if he was an ascetic or a *Bairagi*, Vaishnava, Hindu or Muslim, Khatri or Brahmin, Vaishya or Sudra. They asked him, 'O Beloved of God! What is your dress and what do you eat? Also please let us know about yourself so that we can make out as to what should be your diet and could serve you appropriately'. In reply to it, the Guru uttered the following hymn (*shabad*):

> *They, who make truth their fasting, contentment their pilgrim-station, cognition and meditation their ablution,*
>
> *Compassion their deity and forgiveness their rosary; the most sublime are those persons.*
>
> *They, who make the right way their lion-cloth, consciousness their sacred enclosure, good deeds their frontal-mark,*
>
> *and the Lord's love their food; few, very few are such men, O Nanak.*
>
> (Guru Granth Sahib, p. 1245)

When the sadhus listened to these words of the Guru, they fell at his feet. The footsteps of Guru Nanak have been preserved on the hill at Hinglaj and the place is known as *Guru Nanak Kharao*.

Hari Ram Gupta writes that during Maharaja Ranjit Singh's time (1799–1839) the Baluchi tribes were a force to reckon with in the Derajat area in South Punjab. Hari Ram Gupta has given details of the Maharaja's several expeditions and subjugation of these tribes including the Mazaris through battles and diplomacy. At that time, Sindh was ruled by Baluchi chiefs of the Talapur tribe. The Mir brothers who ruled Sindh kept on sending gifts to the Maharaja but avoided giving an annual tribute[4].

Indigenous Hindus

Between the years 1911 to 1931 the Baluchistan Census recorded the Muslims, Hindus and Sikhs as both indigenous and alien. The latter were the immigrants who lived in districts and mainly in the Quetta region. The former lived mainly in princely states. The immigrants from Punjab, Sindh and other Indian provinces were classified as alien.

Sikhs			
Year	**Indigenous**	**Alien**	**Indigenous**
1911	2,799	5,591	33%
1921	841	6,900	11%
1931	48	8,377	0.6%
Hindus			
1911	14,985	22,617	40%
1921	17,479	33,869	34%
1931	16,903	36,778	32%

The Census of Baluchistan in 1931 notes that in relation to people who previously had maintained that they were *Sahajdhari* (Sikhs) had now (in 1931) have declared themselves as Hindus, 'The only link between these persons and the Sikh religion were the Sikh scriptures. They knew little of their own. They read the Sikh scripture but performed other rites in the manner of their brethren in Sindh. A hint from their religious teachers whose visits have become more frequent of late had the desired effect and they almost bodily went back to the religion which they in reality professed'.

The Hindus were categorised in the following castes namely Arora, Gurkha, Khatri, Rajput, Brahman, Arya (Samaji), Depressed classes (scavengers, cobblers, sweepers) and others. The Gurkhas were definitely 'alien', they were part of the Gurkha regiment posted in the province. The report suggests that most of the depressed classes were also 'alien'[5].

In 1941, there were 49,227 (53,681 in 1931) Hindus and 12,044 Sikhs (8,425 in 1931 Census) in Baluchistan constituting 6.34 percent and 1.4 percent of the total population of the province. In terms of Sikhs, the Census notes '(Sikhs) have made sustained and systematic efforts to bring the members of their community under strict religious control. The appreciable increase in the number of the *Keshdharis* though only at the cost of the *Sahajdharis* shows plainly enough that their efforts have not been fruitless'.

Year	*Keshdhari*	*Sahajdhari*
1911	4,013	3,117
1921	5,013	1,130
1931	7,469	773

Both Hindu and Sikh leaders made some efforts to bring people into their fold. In the former case, a lot of people started to put themselves as Hindus in the census but did not stop reading *Gurbani*. In the latter case, many *Sahajdhari* Sikhs took *Khande di Pahul* and became Khalsa Sikh.

Present situation

The provisional 2017 census of Baluchistan stated that there were 74,040 Hindus and formed 0.6 percent of the population of the province. As per the last census in

1998, the Hindus were about 39,000. There was some migration of Hindus due to law and order situation and economic reasons but it seems that it has been minimal. Similar to the Hindus of North Sindh, the majority of Hindus in Baluchistan also have a dual belief system which is a combination of Sikh and Hindu religions. They go to Hindu temples and undertake idol worship but also recite compositions from the Guru Granth Sahib. However, there is a small minority who call themselves *Gursikhs* and are essentially *Sahajdhari*. They believe in the ten Gurus and the Guru Granth Sahib only and do not practice idol worship. In very few cases, some of these *Gursikhs* or *Sahajdharis* have taken *Khande di Pahul* and are now Khalsa Sikhs. There are at least five functional Gurdwaras in Baluchistan where the vast majority of *Sangat* is non-Khalsa Sikhs. There are a number of small Mandirs across Baluchistan. At a few places, Gurdwaras and Mandirs are on the same premises but have different buildings.

Quetta, the capital of Baluchistan is the main city of the province. Almost one-third of the state's population lives in the Quetta division. There were three or four Gurdwaras in the city before partition but the Sikhs faced such a fury of violence that all of them left for India (like most Hindus). One of the old Gurdwaras now houses a school. The city still has roads named after the Sikhs and Hindus who were once a part and parcel of the city. Some of these roads are Gurdat Singh Road, Moti Ram Road, Patel Road, Tola Ram Road and Nahta Singh Street.

The *Sikh Encyclopaedia* mentions that the city of Quetta hosted several prominent Sikhs who lived there for many years before partition. Among them were Babu Labh Singh (d. 1947), freedom fighter and Akali leader, former *Akal Takht Jathedar* Sadhu Singh Bhaura (d. 1984) and Dr Jaswant Singh Neki (d. 2015). Gadarite Hira Singh (d. 1929) came to Baluchistan and Sindh to incite revolt among the local people.

A few years ago, a Gurdwara was built in the Quetta Cantonment area. There are at least four functional Mandirs in Quetta. One place of worship has the Guru Granth Sahib placed with utmost reverence. There is daily *Keertan* of *Asa di Waar* in the morning and *Nitnem* is performed too. In the other room, a Shiv *Lingam* is installed. There are less than ten Sikh (Khalsa) families in the capital.

The district of Chagai that borders Iran and Afghanistan has a Gurdwara Sahib in the sub-division of Dalbandian. The population has 800 Hindus and around twenty Sikhs (Khalsa) but almost all believe in the Guru Granth Sahib and go to the Gurdwara. The Sikhs converted from being *Sahajdhari* Sikhs who like in Sindh call themselves *Gursikhs*. The *Keertan* is performed by *Sahajdhari* Sikhs. There are two *birs* of the Guru Granth Sahib, one in Gurmukhi and the other in Sindhi (Persian-Arabic script).

All *Gurpurabs* are celebrated with great fervour by the *Sangat*. The premises also have a Lal Sain or Jhule Lal temple but it is in a separate building. These two are the only Hindu and Sikh places of worship in the whole city.

One of biggest producers of rice, Usta Mohammad is a city and sub-division of the Jafarabad district of

Baluchistan. There are about 1,000 Hindus and almost 700 of them are *Guru Nanak Naam Leva Sikhs*[7]. There are about fifty Sikhs (Khalsa) here. The city has a Gurdwara Sahib. Further north, Dera Allah Yar in Jaffarabad district also has Gurdwara Sahib and a minor population of *Sahajdhari* Sikhs.

Dera Murad Jamali is a city in Nasirabad district of Baluchistan and is about sixty kilometres further from Usta Mohammad. The town has a population of 1,200–1,500 Hindus. The city has a small Gurdwara by the name of Baba Guru Nanak Sikh Sabha Gurdwara. The *Sangat* consists of 350 people and consists entirely of *Guru Nanak Naam Leva Sikhs*.

Most of the Hindus in Baluchistan are from the trader caste and have the following surnames: Pahuja, Ahuja, Sukhijia, Matray, Makhija, Kataria, Kukreja, Rahija, Bajaj, Sachdev, Sharma, Sidhana and Sandoria, etc.

In the 1931 census, 27 percent of the population had declared Pashto and 34 percent declared Balochi as their first language. According to the 1998 census, 30 percent of the people in the province spoke Pashto which was not surprising as the Pathans form a major chunk of the population while 55 percent recorded their first language as Balochi. Sindhi had decreased from 18 percent to 5.6 percent during this period. Interestingly, the dialects of Punjabi have been able to maintain their numbers. Lahnda which is a western Punjabi dialect was spoken by 4 percent in 1931. In 1998, Punjabi and Seraiki were spoken by 2.5 percent and 2.4 percent of the population respectively.

In Quetta, the language spoken in the city is Pashto (and Urdu) while in Dalbandian it is Balochi (and Urdu). Most of the Hindus and Sikhs in Baluchistan are multi-lingual. They speak Balochi, Pashto and Urdu with ease. However, most of them speak Seraiki or Sindhi at home. Seraiki is a sister language of Punjabi and spoken in Multan and its neighbouring areas. However, the dialect of Seraiki spoken in Baluchistan is a bit different than that spoken in Multan. Most Hindus in Kalat speak Sindhi at home. It is quite possible that these people came to Baluchistan from that area a few hundred years ago.

Baluchistan is a desert and sparingly populated and it is quite possible that a number of Hindus never left the province especially those living in isolated and small places. Following the migration of the Hindus from Multan area a few hundred years ago, the locals after a time, took the language of the immigrant Hindus as they were in majority (see indigenous and alien numbers in 1911–31). This is a plausible theory. We know that in Kalat, Sindhi Hindus came at the behest of the local ruler and migrants soon became the majority.

A similar thing happened with the Sikhs in the Indian state of Jammu and Kashmir who have lived there for 500 years and few of them are even ethnically Kashmiri but now all of them speak Punjabi (eastern dialect). Even the ones who migrated in 1947 from the now 'Pakistani-administered Kashmir' who originally spoke Hindko now speak Punjabi (eastern dialect). Eventually, the minority indigenous community mingles and identifies with the language of the co-religionists who are superior in numbers.

The Hindus and Sikhs in Baluchistan have mostly been untouched by the change in dynamics of the Hindu-Sikh relations in post-independent India. They continue (almost) living together the same way they did before partition. They are present in a number of towns but they are a minuscule minority. Most of them are shopkeepers and small businessman but there are Hindu doctors as well. The Sikhs (Khalsa) are very few and most, if not all, converted in the past fifteen years or so. A number of Gurdwaras have been built in the past couple of decades. The Gurdwaras which were abandoned in 1947 have been lost like elsewhere in Pakistan but the community is resilient and still surviving.

References

1. Henry Pottinger. (1810). *Travels in Beloochistan and Sinde*. London: Longman.
2. Charles Masson. (1844). *Narrative of Various Journeys in Balochistan, Afghanistan and the Panjab*. London: Richard Bentley.
3. Kirpal Singh. (1969). *Janamsakhi Parampara*. Patiala: Punjabi University.
4. Hari Ram Gupta. (1991). *The History of the Sikhs, Vol. 5: Maharaja Ranjit Singh*. New Delhi: Munshiram Manoharlal Publishers.
5. Gul Muhammad Khan. (1934). *Census of India 1931, Vol. IV: Baluchistan Part 1 and* 2. Lahore.

6. E.H. Gastrell. (1942). *Census of India 1941, Vol. IV: Baluchistan Part 1 and 2*. Lahore.
7. Literally, Sikhs of Guru Nanak. The term is used for *Sahajdhari* Sikhs.

* Information on Baloch Hindus and Sikhs has been procured from a number of native people but due to the poor law and order situation in the province, the names of individuals have not been shared.

19

Hindus, Sahajdharis and Sikhs in Frontier Province (Pakistan)

The North West Frontier Province of Pakistan which borders Afghanistan is a Pashtun majority area but non-Pashtun tribes like Hazarwadi (people of Hazara) are an appreciable minority. The region shares social, cultural and religious ties with Afghanistan. The province was renamed Khyber Pakhtunkhwa (shortened as KPK, land of Pashtuns) in 2010.

The Hindu Shahi ruler Jayapala held Peshawar till 1001 AD when it was lost to Mahmud Ghaznavi. Charles Forster while passing through Peshawar in 1783 records the presence of a number of Hindu shops in the city and states that the Mughal Emperor Akbar (1556–1605) brought a number of Punjabi Muslims and Hindus to Peshawar to encourage trade when the Mughal ruler made new bazaars in the Peshawar city. During the reign of Timur Shah Durrani (1772–93), Ghulam Muhammad who passed through the region records the Hindu grocery shops in Khairabad (in Naushera district)[1].

The region of Hazara is in the North-Eastern part of the Khyber Pakhtunkhwa province of Pakistan. It is located east of the Indus River and comprises seven districts namely Abbottabad, Battagram, Haripur,

Mansehra, Upper Kohistan, Lower Kohistan, and Torghar. When the province was renamed to KPK, it led to violent protests by the Hazara community. Hindus have been living in the region for many centuries.

Somewhere around 1770, Subah Khan Tanoli held a *Jirga* (tribal assembly) to determine how to increase trade in Tanawal and bring it at par with the surrounding regions. The best strategy was determined to be settling the Hindu and Sikh merchants in the town of Bir in Tanawal. Later, most of these families migrated to Haripur and Abbottabad. The local tribal communities recognised the competence of the Sikhs and Hindus in bringing development[2].

The Federal Administered Territory Area (FATA) is a semi-autonomous tribal region in north-western Pakistan almost entirely consisting of Pathans. It is being merged with the neighbouring province Khyber Pakhtunkhwa, in a planned way from 2018–20. It is divided into different agencies (instead of districts). They are as follows:

1. Bajaur Agency
2. Mohmand Agency
3. Khyber Agency
4. Orakzai Agency
5. Kurram Agency
6. North Waziristan Agency
7. South Waziristan Agency.

Guru Nanak travelled from Kabul to Peshawar through Kurram Agency in FATA which was the commonly used route. A few Gurdwaras in the Agency existed till 1947[3]. The *Peshawari Singh Sewa Society* confirmed the existence of Gurdwara Tala Sahib and Thara Sahib in the region commemorating the visit of Guru Nanak in the area. These Gurdwaras were closed after partition but were re-opened in 2017. The said Sewa Society is at the forefront of renovating and repairing of these Gurdwaras. The area has been invested in Taliban attacks for the past few years but relative peace has been achieved now. Only a handful of Khalsa and *Sahajdhari* Sikh families live in the area who take care of the Gurdwaras[4].

Gurdwara Tala Sahib is at Malikhel in Upper Kurram Agency near Malana Dam and Gurdwara Thara Sahib is in the village Ibrahim Zahi. The *Sangat* had created a small memorial and then in 1823 at the request of local *Sangat*, Bhai Rattan Singh of Khadur Sahib sent his son Bhai Sukha Singh who preached the Sikh doctrine and established a beautiful Darbar. When Guru Nanak reached Ibrahim Zahi, the *Sangat* took great care of the Guru and later established Gurdwara Kotha Sahib here to commemorate his visit. This Gurdwara no longer exists (post-1947 scenario) but the said *Sewa Society* has re-established the Gurdwara Thara Sahib in the village[5].

Almost all the Sikhs in KPK and Punjab province in Pakistan can trace their lineage from FATA, the area which escaped the communal violence which engulfed the subcontinent in 1947. Their remarkable story is added later in the book.

The Sikh religion was introduced in the region by Guru Nanak. Some Sikhs would have settled when Maharaja Ranjit Singh first won Peshawar in 1818 and later annexed it in 1834. A number of Gurdwaras were established and every town had at least one Sikh place of worship. The *Sikh Encyclopaedia* records Singh Sabha Gurdwaras established in Haripur (1886), Kohat (1886–87), Loralai (1903) and Peshawar (1905) among others. *Shiromani Khalsa Diwan,* a Sikh socio-political organisation was formed in the 1920s by Jagat Singh Narag, a Peshawar-based businessman, who later became the member of the provisional legislative assembly. All *Singh Sabha Gurdwaras* in the province were affiliated to the *Chief Khalsa Diwan* at Amritsar[6].

In addition to George Forster (1783), the 1931 Census notes the presence of Hindus prior to the Maharaja, 'The Saddozai Nawabs, who ruled it, as well as part of Bannu, until overthrown by the Sikhs, commonly employed Hindus as generals and governors, and it was in the hands of a Hindu, Diwan Daulat Rai, that it was left by the Sikhs'[7].

As per the 1931 Census, there were 156,628 Hindus and 47,935 Sikhs in NWFP (including agencies) forming 6 percent and 1 percent respectively of the total population. Interestingly, the Bannu municipality town was a Hindu majority. The Abbottabad Cantonment was also a Hindu majority town but solely due to the permanent posting of the Gurkha regiment. The Hindus and Sikhs were the money-lending, trading and clerical classes.

The census refers to indigenous Sikhs who were traders like the Hindus. But considerable proportions were immigrants who were in the army or government service. Interestingly as per the 1931 Census, both groups spoke Hindko, a western dialect of Punjabi. As the population of Sikhs was low in FATA, their number was stated but their language was not mentioned separately.

Small minorities with common culture tend to stick together and the census made a note of it, 'They (Hindus and Sikhs) bind themselves together by the artificial ties which they feel they require as a minority, and which are of even more force in their own minds than the ties of religion by which they are bound together in the minds of outsiders (Muslims)'.

By the next census, the population of Hindus and Sikhs had increased. The census of 1941 records 197,631 Hindus and 62,411 Sikhs in the province constituting 6.4 percent and 2 percent of the total population. About 26 percent of all Hindus and 38 percent of all Sikhs lived in Peshawar district. Out of these a small proportion lived in the FATA area namely 17,310 Hindus and 4,472 Sikhs[8].

The *Sikh Encyclopaedia* interestingly states that Sikhs were businessmen and professionals but a fair number were also farmers mainly in the Hazara district. In the provincial assembly, nine and three seats were reserved for Hindus and Sikhs respectively out of the fifty before partition and the *Shiromani Khalsa Diwan* candidates won the elections. The majority of Sikhs and Hindus left the province for India during the partition. A few thousand crossed over to Afghanistan due to their proximity to the border.

At present, there are about 8,000 Khalsa Sikhs in the capital Peshawar. Five years ago their numbers were double but kidnapping, extortion and killing of prominent Sikhs have forced them to settle in the West Punjab. The Pakistani census does not record the number of Sikhs separately on census forms. The Sikhs raised this issue in 2017 at the provincial High Courts but the census department managed to scrape through as they pleaded that they have already printed millions of forms and it would require a lot of time, effort and money to print new forms.

The population by religion percentage released by the Pakistan Bureau of Statistics states that there are 0.08 percent of 'Others' in KPK and 0.07 percent in FATA which constitute 24,416 and 3,500 respectively. This approximates to 28,000 people which is the number of Sikhs, Kalash, Bahai and other small denominations combined[9]. The vast majority of them are Sikhs and it could be safely said that there are about 15,000 Sikhs in KPK (and FATA). This includes the *Sahajdhari* Sikhs. Unlike in Sindh and Baluchistan, the *Sahajdhari* Sikhs in KPK put their religion as Sikhs in the census.

The vast majority of the Khalsa Sikhs are from Khatri and Arora (trader castes) background. The common surnames found among them are Gujral, Khanna, Chabbra, Nirmani and Vasdeo.

There are two main Gurdwaras in Peshawar namely Gurdwara Bhai Joga Singh and Gurdwara Bhai Biba Singh. The former was re-opened in 1978 and later was re-opened in 2016. There is a small Gurdwara in RA Bazar as well which was opened in 2017. A few old Gurdwaras are no longer with the Sikh community including the Gurdwara in Gor Khatri commemorating the visit of Guru Nanak built by his son Baba Sri Chand as a *Dharamsaal* which was abandoned in 1947. It was demolished and a girls' school has been functioning on the site since many decades.

In addition to Pashto-speaking Khalsa Sikhs, there are about 350 houses of *Sahajdhari* Sikhs living in various towns across the province. The town of Mingora in Swat has about eighty houses with two Gurdwaras. Dr Gyan Prakash, a paediatrician, Dr Amreek Lal, a pathologist and Prof. (Retired) Radhe Sham are few eminent professionals from the community.

Other towns with *Sahajdhari* population are Ghurghusti, Chingli, Pirbaba, Khwazakhela, Mardan, Hungu and Bannu among others[10]. These towns have local Singh Sabha Gurdwaras. Many youngsters have taken *Khande di Pahul* and become Khalsa. They have the following surnames Malhotra, Sethi, Makol, Chopra, Jaggi, Kakar, Uppal, Ghai, Makhija, Chawla and Longani. All are from the Khatri and Arora background.

In addition, there is a small community which continues with the dual belief system. Interestingly, they are called *Sevaks* as in Afghanistan. They have great faith in Peer Rattan Nath but also visit Gurdwaras and recite the *Gurbani*. They are mostly Khatris with surnames of Chawla and Longani[11].

The population by religion percentage released by the Pakistan Bureau of Statistics of 2017 census states that there were 0.03 percent Hindus in KPK and 0.06 percent in FATA which constitutes 9,162 and 3,000 people respectively. The total comes out to 12,162.

The majority of these Hindus belong to the Valmiki sect, they worship Valmik, the bandit turned saint author of the holy book *Ramayana,* as God. With the exception of this, they follow mainstream Hinduism which includes idol worship and reverence to various gods and goddesses especially Lord Shiva, Shri Ram, Shri Krishna, Goddesses Durga and Kali. They are included in the Scheduled Castes (in India) and found mostly in the Indian states of Punjab and Uttar Pradesh.

Being such a small minority, their status is a bit better than their Indian counterparts and many are educated. Most of them go to Gurdwaras as well. A small number of Valmiki Hindus have taken *Khande di Pahul* and become Khalsa Sikhs. They have built a small Gurdwara at RA Bazaar in Peshawar Cantonment. The Sikhs and Hindus from the Valmiki background are fighting a court case regarding the possession of their 'place of worship' in Peshawar Cantonment. The relations between them are intertwined as sometimes one brother is Khalsa Sikh but the other is a 'Hindu' who also recites the *Gurbani* in addition to Hindu religious texts. Like the Afghan Hindus, the KPK Hindus cover their heads in Mandirs and do *Ardas*.

The capital Peshawar which has about 2,500 Hindus has three main functional Mandirs. They are as follows:

Gorakhnath Mandir: The Mandir dedicated to Gorakhnath, the founder of Yogi Cult, was re-opened in 2011 and is located at Gor Khatri in Peshawar. The archaeology board outside the temple states that the Mandir was built during the Sikh occupation of Peshawar from 1834–49.

Kali Bari Mandir: The Mandir is dedicated to Goddess Kali. The word *Bari* means elder sister. Puja is performed every Tuesday. A big painting of Saint Valmiki is drawn on the inside wall of the Mandir.

Dargah Peer Rattan Nath Mandir: It is dedicated to Yogi Rattan Nath. There are Dargah Peer Rattan Nath Mandirs in Afghanistan and one in Kurram Agency. A goat is sacrificed on *Shivratri* (Lord Shiva's day) and the cooked meat is served to the congregation on this day.

There is a small Valmiki Mandir in Peshawar as well.

Asamai Mandir: This is a non-functional Mandir in a ruinous state and was in news recently as the ETPB had 'sold' it to a private builder who intended to build a shopping complex on the site. There is an Asamai Mandir in Kabul as well.

The Shiv Mandir in Mansehra with a white marble Shiv *lingam* was renovated recently. It is said to be about 800 years old and some date it to the pre-Islamic era[12].

Naushera has six Mandirs. There are Mandirs in Kohat, Hangu, Bannu, Mardan, Pir Baba, Buner and Dera Ismail Khan[13].

Ram Takht atop the Mount Elum, 9,200 feet above sea level, in Buner district is a sacred pilgrimage for Hindus who call it Ram Takht (throne of Sri Ram). The locals call it Jogian Sar (Peak of the Jogis) as before partition, Hindu ascetics would come to meditate and some would remain on site for all year round. It is said that Ram Chandra, the Hindu God came here and meditated during his exile. The temple and monastery are in ruins but the site is still visited by Hindus in the month of *Savan* (July–August)[14].

The footprints of the Hindu past could be found elsewhere as well. There is a *ziarat* (final resting place) in village Gujjar Bhandi near Mansehra called *Seeni Dadi de Ziarat*. *Seeni* means female leopard in Hindko, the local language. *Dadi* means paternal grandmother but in olden times the term was used out of respect to any old lady in the village. The folklore states that this woman saint rode on a leopard, had snakes around her neck (like a necklace) and went around the area punishing evil spirits, demons, and djinns[15]. The village is inhabited by Gujjars, pastoral agricultural ethnic group who are found across the Indian sub-continent, almost entirely Muslim in Pakistan and both Hindu and Muslim in India. The description is similar to Durga or Shakti, the Hindu Goddess depicted as riding a tiger in India. The tiger is indigenous to India and leopard is found in the mountainous regions of KPK. One may conclude that these Gujjars converted from Hinduism to Islam but continued to revere their old deity but in a slightly modified form.

References

1. Robert Nichols. (2001). *Settling the Frontier Land, Law, and Society in the Peshawar Valley, 1500–1900*. Islamabad: Oxford University Press.
2. Sayyad Murad Ali Aligarhi. (1875). *Tareekh e Tanolian, Maktaba Qadriyya Jamiyyeh Nizamiya Rizviya, Andrun*. Lahore. (Jahandad Khan Tanoli brought this Urdu source to attention).
3. Kirpal Singh. (1969). *Janamsakhi Parampara*. Patiala: Punjabi University.
4. Information provided by Gurpal Singh and Charanjeet Singh of *Peshawari Singh Seva Society*.
5. Information provided by Charanjeet Singh and Gurpal Singh of *Peshawari Singh Seva Society*.
6. Harbans Singh. (1992). *The Encyclopaedia of Sikhism*. Patiala: Punjabi University.
7. Captain G.L. Mallam and A.D.F. Dundas. (1933). *Census of India 1931 Vol 15, North-West Frontier Province*, Peshawar.
8. *Census of India 1941 Vol 15, North-West Frontier Province*, Peshawar.
9. http://www.pbs.gov.pk/content/population-religion. Accessed on 7th August 2018.
10. Information provided by Harmeet Singh, a Sahajdhari Sikh from Bannu, his brother has become a Khalsa-Sikh.
11. Information provided by Bhai Bansri Lal, Granthi and Keertaniya of Mingora Gurdwara, Swat (KPK).

12. Information provided by Shahid Shabbir, Pakistan Heritage Club.
13. Information provided by Avinash Das from Peshawar.
14. https://tribune.com.pk/story/1602881/10-losing-your-religion/. Accessed on 21st August 2018.
15. Information provided by Jahandad Khan Tanoli.

20

The 'Pathan Sikhs' of Pakistan

The Pashtun tribe is popularly known as Pathans in Pakistan but they share the cultural and social ties with the co-tribes across the border in Pakistan. The Pashto-speaking Sikhs of Peshawar (capital of Khyber Pakhtunkhwa province) are a fascinating lot. All the Sikhs settled in the towns of Hasan Abdal (Panja Sahib), Nankana Sahib and rest of West Punjab know that their grandparents came from the FATA area. These Sikhs may be known as 'Pathan Sikhs' in India or West but the local Pathans (Muslims) do not consider them as either indigenous or Pathan. They are considered as 'honoured guests' as a tribal law hence, outsiders. Their education and upbringing does not allow them to even consider that a Pathan can be anything but Muslim[1].

The local Pathans consider that the Sikhs (and Hindus) came to Peshawar and the region when Maharaja Ranjit Singh annexed the Peshawar province in 1834. This theory is easily debunked as George Forster (1783) and Elphinstone (1808) both noted Hindus and Sikhs in the region. Prior to them, Babur and Jahangir, the Mughal rulers note Hindu yogis and ascetics in Gor Khatri area of Peshawar. The Hindus and Sikhs of Afghanistan and KPK province share surnames and almost all of them are Arora and Khatri sub-castes (traders and mercantile castes). During the medieval era, the Hindus of Afghanistan and this region became *Nanakpanthis* and later Khalsa.

In a short history spanning seventy-one years, Pakistan had a mixed relationship with the Sikhs, going from one extreme to another. In Pakistan, there is a general belief, especially among Punjabi Muslims that the Sikhs killed Muslims during partition riots. The fascinating thing is that they think only the Sikhs killed them (as Hindus are incapable or not brave enough to kill Muslims). The riots in East Punjab started when the Sikhs and Hindus started coming from West Punjab in August 1947. Based on this belief, West Punjab became 'Sikh free' and almost 'Hindu-free'. The Government of India had to send a Sikh priest on a six-month visa to look after the Gurdwara Janam Asthan in Nankana Sahib, the birthplace of Guru Nanak. The few unfortunate Sikhs, who remained in West Punjab, in the hope that eventually things would improve, had to convert. The Sikh Jats who shared the surname with Muslim Jats took Islam and the lower castes converted to Christianity. The Christian community did not migrate and suffered during the partition riots. A few Punjabi Muslims and Christians in West Punjab admit privately about their grandfathers being Sikhs[2].

The situation was so bad for the Sikhs that even in Sindh where not more than twenty Hindus were killed, the Sikhs were rounded up in a Gurdwara in Karachi, the doors closed and the Gurdwara was set on fire. Over 1,000 Sindhi Sikhs who had no hand in killing any Muslim were killed in cold blood by the Muslim refugees[3]. In interior Sindh, the Rajput Hindu princely state of Umerkot acceded to Pakistan and the neighbouring district of Tharparkar which had a Hindu majority (even today 40% of the population is Hindu) saw almost no Hindu emigration to India unlike the rest of the Sindh. The last of the Sikhs left Tharparkar along with some Brahmin families after the 1971 war[4].

Coming back to 1947, the vast majority of the Sikhs (and Hindus) in Frontier province left for India. Some went to Afghanistan and then to Iran and took the sea route to India. About 2,000–3,000 settled in Afghanistan. Some Sikhs took refuge in the basement of Bhai Joga Singh Gurdwara in Peshawar. Some later cut their hair but continued to follow the Sikh religion in private. A *Sahajdhari* Sikh reveals that though their grandfathers and great-grandfathers were Khalsa Sikhs, they had to cut their hair and remove their turbans to survive. Almost four generations later they have again taken up the *Khande di Pahul* and become Khalsa.

The Sikhs living in FATA did not face any such issues in 1947 due to their remote location, it was not before a good few months had elapsed that they came to know about the partition. Probably about six months after the partition, the Sikhs in FATA decided to leave and came as far as Rawalpindi, the western border of West Punjab and realised that there was a lot of anger among the local people against Sikhs and there was no way they would survive a journey to the Indian border. It was agreed that the Sikhs would go back to their respective agencies and pay tax (*Jizya*) or protection money for the time being.

In October–November 1969 the Sikhs all over the world celebrated 500 years of the birth anniversary of Guru Nanak. To commemorate the pious event, Ishar Singh and his extended family came to Nankana Sahib. The Gurdwara Janam Asthan, the birthplace of Guru Nanak was in a very bad state then. He did *Ardas* and pledged to the Almighty that he would wrap up his businesses in FATA and settle in Nankana Sahib for good. A couple of families decided to stay in Nankana Sahib and the rest went back to Kurram Agency with an intention to wrap up their businesses. The only Sikh in the Gurdwara and the Nankana Sahib town was Giani Partap Singh who in 1965 had destroyed his Indian passport when following the 1965 war, Pakistan had decided to stop the arrangement for procuring an Indian Sikh priest for Gurdwara Janam Asthan on a half-yearly visa. The Giani could foresee that the only functional Gurdwara in West Punjab which happens to be one of the most important ones will fall into shambles if no Sikh caretaker was available. This exceptional person taught Gurmukhi to the Pashto-speaking FATA Sikhs and died in Pakistan but not before passing on the Sikh tenets, *Gurbani* and script to the FATA Sikhs.

Meanwhile, Ishar Singh's extended family started to wrap up their business. As they were also moneylenders they started asking locals to clear up their debt which created some animosity against the family. In December 1971, in a short war, India defeated Pakistan and East Pakistan became a new country called Bangladesh.

The famous photograph of Pakistani General Niazi surrendering to Indian General Jagjit Singh Arora was not lost to the locals as the Pathans formed a major chunk of the Pakistani Army. The Sikhs were blamed for the defeat and using this as a pretext the locals arrested the extended family of Ishar Singh in Kurram Agency and forcibly cut the hair of Sikh men and made them hostages. When after a few months this was reported to the family in Nankana Sahib, Ishar Singh and his brother Aaya Singh came to Kurram Agency but were not allowed to meet the family.

Ishar Singh decided to approach a number of people back in Punjab. An influential Muslim lady in Rawalpindi who was helped by the Sikhs during the 1947 partition riots spoke to people in authority and they were assured of assistance once they were in mainland Pakistan. FATA was autonomous and the Pakistani authorities were unable to intervene. Ishar Singh, his son Ajit and his brother Aaya went back to Kurram Agency and tried to win over the locals by paying money. They involved the local *Jirga* and a few people who were sympathetic but they were declined permission to meet their wives and children. In despair, Ishar Singh, his son and his brother allowed their hair to be cut as it was the only way to see their families. After staying there for a year and winning their confidence, one night after careful planning the whole family left Kurram Agency and came to West Punjab. Through the same influential lady in Rawalpindi, they filed a petition in court to rescue them from this ordeal. This forced the village elders to come to an agreement.

The Sikhs were asked to leave and never come back to the village. It was agreed (or imposed) that the villagers (in Kurram Agency) would not bother Ishar Singh's extended family and he would withdraw the court case. Ishar Singh and his family had to leave all their land, orchards and house behind just like millions across both sides left after the partition of Punjab.

In 1973, Ishar Singh and his extended family, which consisted of seven nuclear families, settled in the Nankana Sahib town. This raised alarm bells among some of the local and powerful individuals who saw them as major obstacle lest the Sikhs demanded the thousands of acres of land associated with the Gurdwara Janam Asthan. Maharaja Ranjit Singh (1799–1839) had allotted land to the Gurdwaras so that they were economically self-reliant in managing their affairs. However, in case of Nankana Sahib, Rai Bhular Bhatti, the local chief and devotee of Guru Nanak had given more than half of his property in name of the holy saint. Due to this 'fear', the local Muslims made life difficult for the Sikh families here. These powerful locals filed a case against Ishar Singh's extended family which discouraged other Sikhs in FATA to come over to Nankana Sahib. The local Muslims lost the case in the Session Court and also in the High Court. They appealed in Supreme Court in 1992 but later withdrew their case. They were told that they were cultivating the land and nobody was taking away from them but that the land should remain in the name of Baba Guru Nanak.

All this time, Ishar Singh and his wife Tarn Kaur dedicated their lives and took care of the Gurdwara

Janam Asthan. In 1989, Sikhs from abroad (Western countries) visited Nanakana Sahib and were upset at the state of the Gurdwara buildings and requested the ETPB to take care of them. The local Sikhs particularly remember the renovations of Gurdwaras under the tenure of a Christian Chairman of ETPB. In 1999, Pakistan decided to create the *Pakistan Sikh Gurdwara Parbandak Committee* (Management Committee) which marked the tercentenary anniversary of Khalsa. Ishar Singh's son Ajit Singh opened the first Gurmukhi School in 1999, his cousin and son of Aaya Singh, Mastaan Singh opened a Sikh public school in the town and later became the first Sikh Councillor in Pakistan.

By this time, the Taliban were quite active in FATA and the number of Sikhs who were waiting for an opportunity to leave, came to Nankana Sahib. By 2002 there were fifty Sikh families in Nankana Sahib. After 2006, a few *Sahajdhari* Sikh families affected by the poor law and order situation in Baluchistan came to Nankana Sahib and became Khalsa too. In 2009 and 2010, several Sikh families left FATA as the Taliban demanded *Jizya* and beheaded a Sikh youngster. At present, there are about 400 Sikh families in Nankana Sahib and about 150 in Hasan Abdal (Panja Sahib).

A local Muslim man from Nankana Sahib went to Australia about ten or fifteen years ago for higher education. He was invited for dinner by the local Sikh family as he came from the 'holy land' of Nankana Sahib. When he told his host that he was a Bhatti Muslim and came from the family of Rai Bular Bhatti, he was given a huge welcome. A number of local Sikh households invited him to their houses. The Sikhs cherish the memories of all those who were close to their Gurus. The Bhatti-Sikh association was re-established (post-1992 when the case was withdrawn) and since then every year the local Bhatti family, direct descendants of Rai Bhular, joins Guru Nanak's *Gurpurab* celebrations.

Peshawar

After the 1971 war, Sikhs started leaving FATA and came to Peshawar, and this swelled their numbers. They sent a deputation to the authorities to allow the re-opening of their Gurdwaras. In 1978, General Zia, the President of Pakistan allowed the re-opening of Bhai Joga Singh Gurdwara, a historic Gurdwara commemorating one of the close Sikhs of the last Guru, Gobind Singh[5].

Khurana provides a bit of history of Bhai Joga Singh Gurdwara which gives a flavour of the challenges the Sikhs had to face in Peshawar. During the Durrani era (later half of the 18th century), the ruling elite proclaimed that the site of the Gurdwara was a *ziarat* (final resting place) of Jogan Shah, a Muslim fakir. The daughter of the Afghan Governor of Peshawar had recovered after seeking blessing at this Gurdwara. This increased the prestige of the Gurdwara in the eyes of the local Muslims who started to come to the Gurdwara in great numbers much to the chagrin of the Governor who then declared it to be the *ziarat* of a Muslim fakir!

In the early 20th century, idols were brought in Gurdwara Bhai Joga Singh in Peshawar. The Sikhs of Kabul along with those in Peshawar protested as the Sikh religion believes in one formless Supreme

Reality (God) hence, idol worship was rejected. There were a number of scuffles between the Sikhs and the other group. Ultimately, the two factions signed an agreement on 17th March 1920 and the management of the Gurdwara was transferred to the Sikhs[6]. The street where this Gurdwara is located in Peshawar is still called *Mohalla* Jogan Shah!

Change in dynamics

In the late 1980s and 1990s, the Indian Government imposed sanctions and blacklisted a huge number of Sikhs[7] living abroad for allegedly anti-Indian activities. In many cases, a participation in the rally protesting against the 1984 attack on Harmandar Sahib (Golden Temple) in Amritsar was good enough reason to blacklist a Sikh. For these people, the visit to historic Gurdwaras in Pakistan became a viable and only option instead of East Punjab. Pakistan became a pilgrimage destination especially around the birth anniversary of Guru Nanak. By 1994, the separatist movement in East Punjab, at least the armed struggle had faded away. But it took another decade and a half before most of the blacklisting was removed.

The demolition of the Babri Masjid in Ayodhya considered as 'disputed' by many on 6th December 1992 led to attacks on a number of Mandirs and Gurdwaras in Pakistan. To its credit, Pakistan has renovated some of them. This event changed the perception of the Pakistani public. Till then, the Sikhs were hated for their alleged role in the killing of Muslims in the 1947 partition riots. Strangely, in Pakistan most still believe that Muslims lost more members compared to the Sikhs and Hindus during partition. Their conditioning does not allow them to believe that a Hindu is capable of killing a Muslim. Apparently until the 1971 war, many in Pakistan believed that a Muslim man is equivalent to ten Hindus! Post-1993 which also marked the beginning of cable and satellite channel era in South Asia, people began to evaluate their long pre-conceived ideas which led to a change of behaviour towards the Sikhs.

The Sikhs from India and abroad who visit Pakistan tell about the warmth and huge welcome they receive as a guest. However, there is a mixed story for local Sikhs; some local Muslim shopkeepers have different glasses for Sikhs lest they are tainted! There is no concept of untouchability in Islam but it seems roles have reversed. This untouchability is extended to Hindus and Christians as well. At many places, minorities were expected to carry their utensils and in the absence of it they would be refused food and drink by local shopkeepers. These practices have now decreased substantially. Before partition in West Punjab, the Sikhs and Hindus would not dine with Muslims except in Gurdwaras and Sufi shrines.

In Nankana Sahib, a mosque was built at an unusual height so that it was higher than the Gurdwara Janam Asthan. Pakistan is trying to be a pluralistic and modern democracy, however, its flirtation with communalism from the mid-1970s onwards is proving to be a huge hindrance. The people of the sub-continent aspire for peace and prosperity which cannot be achieved without a stable and secular India and Pakistan.

The resilience of Bhai Ishar Singh and his family is exemplary and give readers some flavour of the remarkable journey of Pathan Sikhs who look after the seven Gurdwaras in Nankana Sahib and the overall twenty-five historical Gurdwaras in West Punjab[8]. Pakistan, from a nation which hated Sikhs and their turbans in 1947 to encouraging Sikhs to settle in Nankana Sahib has come a long way. It has been a welcome change and hopefully, will continue in the future.

References

1. In popular opinion, to be a Pathan, one needed to have Pathan blood. Nobody was able to expand on it but essentially one cannot be a Pathan if s/he is not Muslim even if he or she has lived in the region for centuries.
2. The Punjabi Christian did not suffer in the partition and hence, did not migrate to either East or West Punjab.
3. Gurbachan Singh Talib. (1950). *Muslim League Attack on Sikhs and Hindus in the Punjab 1947*. Amritsar: SGPC.
4. A local Sindhi shared this information in private.
5. *India Today* magazine, April 1999 (Commemorative issue—300 years of Khalsa).
6. Khajinder S. Khurana. (2001). *Kabul de Sangat tee Afghanistan da Sankhep Ithas*. New Delhi.
7. After welcoming Afghan refugees for years, Pakistan has been deporting them for the past few years. Inderpal Singh (Kapoor), a young man of 24 years informs that when he was five years old, his father, Deep Singh with his family left Kabul and came to Pakistan.

They settled in Panja Sahib (Hasan Abdal) and for the next eighteen years he lived and studied there. He was actively involved in the Gurdwara Sahib. In September 2017, the Pakistan government deported them and they went back to Kabul. Following the suicide bombing in Jalalabad (1st July 2018) the family is actively considering moving abroad.

8. https://www.pakistantoday.com.pk/2018/03/11/two-identities-twice-the-pride-the-pashtun-sikhs-of-nankana-saheb/. Accessed on 23rd August 2018.

Appendix

List of Gurdwaras in Afghanistan

The list of Gurdwaras including few Gur Asthan (places visited by Sikh Gurus) has been taken from the book *Ithas Khalsa Diwan Afghanistan*[1]. The local Gurdwaras (and non-historical ones) are usually designated as Singh Sabha Gurdwara named after the late 19th and early 20th century Sikh reform movement.

Name	City	Province
1. Gurdwara Singh Sabha	Lal Pur	Nangarhar
2. Gurdwara Guru Asthan	Pishpulaak	Nangarhar
3. Gurdwara Singh Sabha	Bisoal	Nangarhar
4. Gurdwara Singh Sabha	Sarshahi	Nangarhar
5. Gurdwara Singh Sabha	Kaza (New)	Nangarhar
6. Gurdwara Singh Sabha (old)	Kaza	Nangarhar
7. Gurdwara Singh Sabha	Bala Bagh	Nangarhar
8. Gurdwara Guru Asthan	Sultanpur	Nangarhar
9. Gur Asthan Siri Chashma Sahib	Sultanpur	Nangarhar (Historical)
10. Gurdwara Guru Nanak Darbar	Jalalabad	Nangarhar
11. Gurdwara Guru Tegh Bahadur Sahib	Jalalabad	Nangarhar
12. Gurdwara Singh Sabha	Bilangara	Nangarhar
13. Gurdwara Singh Sabha	Kama	Nangarhar

Name	City	Province
14. Gurdwara Singh Sabha	Bajarak	Nangarhar
15. Gurdwara Singh Sabha	Kalatak	Nangarhar
16. Gurdwara Singh Sabha	Sheva	Nangarhar
17. Gurdwara Singh Sabha	Kalashahi	Nangarhar
18. Gurdwara Singh Sabha	Nurgal	Kunar
19. Gurdwara Singh Sabha	Pushat	Kunar
20. Gurdwara Singh Sabha	Khas Kunar	Kunar
21. Gurdwara Singh Sabha	Alishing	Laghman
22. Gurdwara Singh Sabha	Trigarhi	Laghman
23. Gurdwara Singh Sabha	Mandrohh	Laghman
24. Gurdwara Singh Sabha	Harmal	Laghman
25. Gurdwara Singh Sabha	Char Bagh	Laghman
26. Gurdwara Guru Nanak Dev	Kabul	Kabul (Historical)[2]
27. Gurdwara Guru Har Rai	Kabul	Kabul
28. Gurdwara Khalsa Ji	Kabul	Kabul
29. Gurdwara Baba Phirana	Kabul	Kabul[3]
30. Gurdwara Baba Almast	Kabul	Kabul[4]
31. Gurdwara Baba Khem Singh	Kabul	Kabul
32. Gurdwara Baba Sri Chand	Kabul	Kabul
33. Gurdwara Baba Mansa Singh	Kabul	Kabul
34. Gurdwara Jyoti Saroop	Kabul	Kabul
35. Gurdwara Ganj Baksh	Kabul	Kabul
36. Gurdwara Singh Sabha Karte Parwan	Kabul	Kabul
37. Gurdwara Singh Sabha Barkari Jan	Logar	Logar

Name	City	Province
38. Gurdwara Singh Sabha	Ghazni, new	Ghazni
39. Gurdwara Singh Sabha	Ghazni, old	Ghazni
40. Gurdwara Kotla Sahib	Ghazni	Ghazni
41. Gurdwara Singh Sabha	Khost	Khost
42. Gurdwara Singh Sabha	Gardez	Paktia
43. Gur Asthan Guru Nanak	Chakmunia	Paktia
44. Gurdwara Baba Hari Shah	Kabuli Darwaza	Kandahar
45. Gurdwara Baba Jagdish	Kabuli Darwaza	Kandahar
46. Gurdwara Masandan da	Kabuli Darwaza	Kandahar
47. Gurdwara Chotti Dharamsaal	Shikarpuri Bazaar	Kandahar
48. Gurdwara Barhi Dharamsaal	Shikarpuri Bazaar	Kandahar[5]
49. Gurdwara Singh Sabha	Lashkargah	Lashkargah
50. Gurdwara Singh Sabha	Lashkargah new	Lashkargah
51. Gurdwara Singh Sabha	Tarinkot	Urozgan
52. Gur Asthan Tutam Dara	Tirikot	Parwan
53. Gurdwara Kotha Sahib	Aaka Sarai	Parwan
54. Gur Asthan Baba Karuka	Rege Rawan	Parwan
55. Gur Asthan Siri Dashma Sahib	Ghorband	Parwan
56. Gurdwara Singh Sabha	Zama Laga	Parwan
57. Gurdwara Singh Sabha, old	Charikar	Parwan
58. Gurdwara Singh Sabha	Charikar, new	Parwan

Name	City	Province
59. Gurdwara Singh Sabha	Biland Kalan	Parwan
60. Gurdwara Singh Sabha	Puli Khumri	Baghlan
61. Gurdwara Singh Sabha	Baghlan	Baghlan
62. Gurdwara Singh Sabha	Kunduz	Kunduz
63. Gurdwara Singh Sabha	Khan Abad	Kunduz

References

1. Sadhu Singh Saathi. (1994). *Ithas Khalsa Diwan Afghanistan*. Jalalabad: Parchar Committee Khalsa Diwan Afghanistan. Khajinder Singh Khurana provided the list.
2. This Gurdwara was demolished during the extension of the road in late 1950. Prof. Ganda Singh held Sikhs responsible for not pursuing the case with the Government. Although a few years later when the same thing happened in Jalalabad they actively engaged with the Government and the plan was changed.
3. In 1986 this small Gurdwara Sahib was merged with Gurdwara Guru Har Rai Sahib.
4. Baba Almast was an Udasi priest, he established the Gurdwara Baba Sri Chand. This is a small Gurdwara next to Khalsa Gurdwara in Kabul. Currently, two Sikh families live in it. They perform the *Prakash* of the Guru Granth Sahib.
5. It is dedicated to Baba Sri Chand, founder of Udasi sect and is now known as Gurdwara Baba Sri Chand.

About the Author

Born and brought up in Amritsar, Inderjeet Singh is an immigrant in the UK, currently based in Nottingham, where he lives with his wife and two daughters. He works in the Support Services of a multinational company. History is his passion and he regularly writes articles on little known Sikh and related topics in a semi-academic style for the *Sikhnet* website. His writing style is simple and free flowing so that they could be read widely, without compromising on references. His work has also been published in *Abstract of Sikh Studies* and *The Tibet Journal*. Some of his important work includes 'Sindhi Hindus & Nanakpanthis in Pakistan', 'Sindhi Sikhs' and 'Zorawar Singh's Campaign in Tibet' among others. The articles can be accessed on https://www.sikhnet.com/authors/inderjeet-singh.

Inderjeet can be contacted at:

Email: inderjeet08@yahoo.com

Facebook page: Book: Afghan Hindus & Sikhs—History of 1000 years